IN INFORMATION
SYSTEMS
DEVELOPMENT

PHILIP C. SEMPREVIVO

IN INFORMATION
SYSTEMS
DEVELOPMENT

Yourdon Press
1501 Broadway
New York, New York 10036

Library of Congress Cataloging in Publication Data

Semprevivo, Philip C.
    Teams in information systems development.

    Bibliography: p.
    Includes index.
    1. Management information systems. 2. Work
groups. I. Title.
T58.6.S4   658.4'03   80-50608
ISBN 0-917072-20-0 (pbk.)

The quotation on page 1 is from F.P. Brooks' *Mythical Man-Month,* © 1974, Addison-Wesley Publishing Company, Inc., Chapter 1, page 4. Reprinted with permission.

Printed in the United States of America

Library of Congress Catalog Number 80-50608

ISBN: 0-917072-20-0

This book was set in Times Roman by YOURDON Press, 1501 Broadway, New York, N.Y., using a PDP-11/45 running un-der the UNIX[†] operating system.

[†]UNIX is a registered trademark of Bell Laboratories.

Contents

Acknowledgments

It is only fitting that the introduction to a book on teams contain some mention of the team effort that went into its development. First, my wife, Peggy, who worked as my research associate while engaged in MBA/MIS graduate study, is a major contributor.

Drs. Nancy Howes and Robert Quinn (of the State University of New York at Albany) provided in-depth evaluation of various portions of the text. I am indebted to each of them for their encouragement, guidance, and criticism.

It has been my good fortune over the years to have had truly excellent project leaders working for me. Larry Mulligan and Patricia Panzl (of SUNY at Albany) are to be especially thanked for the contributions they have made to my education about teams.

It is a pleasure to acknowledge Wendy Eakin, Lorie Mayorga, and Barbara Kurek, all of the YOURDON Press staff, for their cooperation throughout the project.

Finally, special notes of thanks are due Janice Wormington (YOURDON) in preparing the final manuscript; Mary Eggleston, who assisted in preparing earlier versions of the text; and my employer, Deloitte Haskins & Sells, who has encouraged me to continue my research on teams and to develop the firm's consulting practice in this area.

August 1980   Philip C. Semprevivo
                                                        New York City

Preface

People and organizational issues have gained recognition in recent years as being at the core of effective information systems development. Of the many strategies that have been proposed in an attempt to address these issues, the team approach has gained the greatest respect and credibility.

Previous writings on the subject of systems development teams have tended to be piecemeal in the sense of addressing only one or a few important issues. This book is intended to present a comprehensive statement about teams and their application to the process of information systems development. It begins with the assumption that the team is an organizational strategy that should be used primarily to improve the effectiveness of systems, user, and management interactions.

A second feature of the book is that it provides a set of practical guidelines for analyzing, evaluating, and improving team performance. This approach reflects my own belief that there is a need to devise new ways of applying relevant organizational research to real-world situations.

Whether one is teaching students about teams or advising systems professionals who are part of a team, there is a need to substantiate one's judgments about factors that influence team effectiveness. The reader should use the many rating and ranking instruments presented in Part II of the book to readily build new methods for quantifying and documenting those subjective judgments that are so critical to effective systems development.

*To Stephanie,
Stephen,
and Philip*

TEAMS

IN INFORMATION
SYSTEMS
DEVELOPMENT

Part I
Introduction

"No scene from prehistory is quite so vivid as that of the mortal struggles of great beasts in the tar pits. In the mind's eye one sees dinosaurs, mammoths, and sabertoothed tigers struggling against the grip of the tar. The fiercer the struggle, the more entangling the tar, and no beast is so strong or so skillful but that he ultimately sinks.

"Large-system programming has over the past decade been such a tar pit, and many great and powerful beasts have thrashed violently in it."

— Frederick P. Brooks, Jr.
The Mythical Man-Month

There was a time when fear of the computer as a sort of dehumanizing agent appeared to be the single greatest challenge to successful use of computing technology in the business world. This early concern that machines might reduce the average workday to a humdrum of button-pushing, and might result in customers and citizens being treated as simply a series of numbers, was not without value. Indeed, the human factor has been essential in shaping the development and application of this new and powerful technology to provide increasingly beneficial services. While there remain vestiges of this concern, dehumanization can no longer be considered the major challenge confronting us.

To the contrary, there is an unprecedented interest today in the application of computing technology to the needs of business. Management and the user community have become more sophisticated in their understanding of technology and, in many instances, are outright supportive of attempts at large-scale systems development. Yet, despite this encouragement and the allocation of vast amounts of resource support, the systems development process has not worked smoothly. In effect, we have begun to discover that the application of this new tech-

1

nology to the dynamics of business is far more complex than the technology itself.

There is growing interest in the use of the systems development team as a strategy for improving the effectiveness of systems development efforts. As a result of early experiences with team approaches, such as the use of chief programmer teams in the late 1960s, we have begun to learn that there are many factors other than technical ones that have an impact on team development, both positively and negatively. While our understanding of these factors is incomplete, considerable progress is being made.

In Chapter 1, we state the kinds of problems that have traditionally plagued development of large-scale information systems, and make the point that people and organizational issues, not technical issues, are at the core of these problems.

In Chapter 2, we explore the rationale behind the recent impetus for using teams, and see how the ways in which technicians work with one another and with management and user communities have begun to evolve into bona fide team approaches. In particular, the experiences gained from experimentation with teams have served to initiate a more realistic and scientifically based approach to their use.

From these early experiments has come the realization that successful use of teams will necessitate that we first learn more about how people interact as members of a team. Chapters 3 and 4 are a first step in filling the current void of information about group behavior as it pertains to systems development teams.

Returning to basics, Chapter 3 describes the team as an organizational entity; explains factors that affect successful use of teams; points out some of the most prevalent kinds of problems that teams experience; and, in general, provides a conceptual frame of reference for viewing the team as a dynamic entity.

In the final chapter of Part I, the focus is on what can be done to maximize team effectiveness. Practical suggestions are made to improve team performance. Perhaps because the data processing profession has historically encouraged individual decision-making, most teams experience difficulty in making group decisions. Consequently, some extended discussion about effective group decision-making has been provided. Finally, the reader is exposed to several strategies used by professional organizational consultants to improve the effectiveness with which a particular team functions.

At the conclusion of Part I, the reader should possess the conceptual understanding of people and organizations as a prerequisite to being able to perform the practice sets contained in Part II of the text.

Computerized Information Systems: Problems and Change | 1

In recent years, a number of interesting speculations have been made to explain why systems development efforts so frequently fall short of our expectations. Specific suggestions also have been offered for structuring a new framework within which systems development can be performed more successfully. Our objectives in this chapter will be to describe the systems development process, the major criticisms of it, and the changes occurring apparently as a consequence of new insights. In so doing, we hope to adequately depict the turbulent environment that has fostered a growing interest in using teams as a strategy for improving the effectiveness of systems development efforts.

1.1 The systems development process

During the early days of business computing, a typical application — for example, a payroll system — might be developed by an individual who understood both the application (payroll) requirements and the computing (hardware and software) requirements. Using this approach worked well then and continues to work well today in certain situations. For example, with specific knowledge and a home-style microcomputer, you can develop many interesting and successful computer applications for your personal and professional use. In these instances, you are the technician, the user, and the manager for each application.

In a complex and dynamic business environment, the approach is, of necessity, quite different. As Orr has pointed out, our thoughts on the application of computing technology have evolved from experience with simple, small systems that could be developed by a single person to complex, large-scale systems that require great quantities of money, time, and people to develop, and that are so plagued with delivery problems that the process has begun to tax the endurance of business organizations everywhere.[1]

3

The process for developing computerized systems began to develop into a more formalized set of procedures in response to this new environment of complex, large-scale systems. While individual writers on the subject may differ in the terminology used or in the number of steps isolated, there is fundamental agreement on the steps to be followed in developing and implementing a new system. For purposes of illustration, we will use the following sequence:

System Development Process

Problem definition
Data collection and analysis
Analysis of system alternatives
Determination of feasibility
Development of system proposal
Pilot or prototype system development
System design
Program development
System implementation
System follow-up[2]

Several factors have influenced the evolution of this ten-step model. First, the amount of computer programming time as a percentage of total systems development time has dramatically decreased. In addition, the variety of activities performed and the overall time and resource requirements for systems development under this ten-step model are greater than simply adding the time and resource requirements for a large number of very small, one-person systems development efforts.

As indicated earlier, differences about what ought to be done in systems development appear to be relatively minor. There is even increasingly widespread agreement on some of the analysis and design tools and techniques to be employed. But if there is so much agreement on the procedural steps to be followed in developing a new system, why do we find so much evidence of failure?

Many attempts to answer this question have focused upon tools and methods employed by technicians. While the acquisition and employment of technical skills, such as the application of the structured techniques in design and programming, have proved beneficial, they do not directly address a much more fundamental issue: how to implement the systems development strategy in a dynamic business organization. Stated perhaps more simply, the issue is that it is one thing to know what steps an organization ought to follow, but quite another to create an environment in which that organization can and will follow those steps.

To a large extent, this book focuses upon where and why organizations experience difficulties in following the generally agreed-upon development strategy, as well as what can be done to create an environment in which greater effectiveness can be achieved. The primary topic is systems development teams, but — and this is important — systems development teams as an organizational strategy to create an environment that can facilitate the process of systems development.

1.2 The perceptions of problems

Different perceptions about why systems development projects frequently fall short of expectations can be grouped into three major categories:

- management skill and involvement

- formal versus informal process

- technical and organizational incompatibility

For each category, we will describe the specific criticisms of the systems development process, and then examine the extent to which these different criticisms may support a growing thread of common concern.

1.2.1 Management skill and involvement

One set of hypotheses about the problems of systems development projects focuses upon the issues of management skill and/or management involvement. Let us look at each issue more closely.

Keider, for one, argues forcefully that sound technical management is frequently wanting in development efforts.[3] While we have all heard the management skill issue raised time and again in various situations, the argument does apply particularly to computer systems development. The route by which most people become managers of large-scale systems projects is infrequently and at times only accidentally associated with the acquisition of management training. Rather, it is more usually the case that the successful computer programmer is first promoted to systems analyst and ultimately to project manager. Frequently, the criterion for selecting this individual is his or her strong technical skills. With little formal training or prior experience in management per se, the project manager understandably experiences difficulties in executing the formal systems development process within the dynamic business organization.

However, all of the blame cannot be leveled at the project manager. If the manager were solely to blame, we would simply have to invest a little extra time and resources into training project managers.

While certainly desirable, such training is not a panacea. Even a dedicated and skilled technical manager can experience problems when higher-level management chooses to display a lack of dedicated involvement in the systems development process.

In 1969, Diebold raised two significant questions about management involvement in the development of information systems: First, Who sets development goals — management or technicians? and second, Has management taken enough time to understand computing so it can realistically evaluate the benefits of computerization?[4] In many organizations, these questions appear to be nearly rhetorical — the answers being that systems goals are set by technicians, and management has little or no knowledge of computing. Indeed, some critics of management are even harsher in their evaluation, claiming that management, in general, has simply failed to involve itself adequately in the development process. Rather, it has opted to create committees, task forces, and other organizational devices that simply serve to place the blame for inevitable failure elsewhere.[5]

Those arguments that focus upon management skill and/or involvement as the primary culprit are pragmatic and are usually presented by those who have had some line-management or consulting responsibility in a data processing organization.* If management skill and/or involvement are deficient, then a change in the situation would appear rational and, indeed, wise. Certainly, the arguments in favor of a change are strong and persuasive — but they do not represent the only point of view, as we shall see in the next two sections.

1.2.2 Formal versus informal process

Should systems development projects be formal or informal? An example of a very formal concept is a Management Information System (MIS). The MIS model, in which each level of its hierarchy contains information suited to the special needs of a particular echelon of management, attempts to formalize the relationship between information and the business organization. There are those who argue that executives do not always (or even frequently) operate in a way that is

---

*For anyone who has had to perform a feasibility study for a large-scale systems development effort, these comments are particularly relevant, since those studies frequently substantiate that new systems development and the cost of computing in general represents a major financial commitment by an organization; and new systems development will result in pervasive changes to the work that people do, how they do that work, and, to some extent, how they organize and interact in getting the job done.

reflected by the formal organization chart; and further, that any information system constructed so as to mirror the bureaucratic, pyramidal structure of the organization is simply out of sync with reality.[6]

What is the reality? In point of fact, both formal and informal systems are at work in an organization. Like the MIS concept, the process of developing new information systems focuses almost totally on the formal organization. In so doing, however, we attempt to develop systems within a formalized frame of reference that is, at best, less than fully useful. At times, these systems will be totally unacceptable to management and to users, who rely heavily on their informal system or ways of doing work.

Argyris has taken an even more specific look at the systems development process.[7] He states that the formal organization emphasis in systems development simply overlooks the behavioral and emotional impact of management information systems. To demonstrate that the development of a management information system can have emotional impact, Argyris asks us to consider the role of a manager in an environment in which the total corporate picture is available at the lower levels of the organization. Even a limited awareness of how information is processed, managed, and controlled within most bureaucratic organizations underscores the importance of the observation that the information system can be seriously threatening to individual managers.

Traditionally, systems personnel have seen their role evolve from that of technical "guru" to one of a developer of products through technology. They admit that early user dissatisfaction resulted, in part, from their own over-zealous, arrogant, and tactless approach to users. Today, they find it frustrating that, despite their new-found emphasis on developing a user product, the old resistance — and, at times, increased user dissatisfaction — are evidenced. They do not realize that with the maturing of technology they are no longer simply the creators of user products, but the developers of systems processes that affect users in most significant ways.[8] Large-scale systems have pervasive impact upon people and organizations. The impact upon people is not simply rational, but also emotional and behavioral in nature. The effects upon organizations are not (or should not be) limited to the formal organization but are extended to include the informal organization as well.

By attending to the arguments that attack the overly rational systems development approaches, we have begun to gain insight into some of the underlying human and organizational complexities that truly differentiate the development of a large-scale, computerized information system from the task of writing a few, limited-scope computer programs so characteristic of the early days of data processing.

The significance of these issues for systems professionals is clear. Rather than focus solely upon the development of technical skills, they must develop a set of interpersonal communication skills to assist them in understanding the implicit as well as the explicit meaning of their observations.[9] As alluded to previously, the traditional criterion for becoming a systems analyst has been demonstrated excellence as a computer programmer. That tradition may have been a significant factor in fostering overly rational approaches to systems development. As systems professionals gain greater knowledge about people and organizational processes, we can expect the overemphasis on the formal structure to diminish.

1.2.3 Technical and organizational incompatibilities

In the previous two sections, the blame for the failure of large-scale systems development efforts clearly fell upon the process itself as it relates to the people and organizations attempting to implement it. While these "process" concerns represent important contributions to our understanding of the problem, there is another, equally important perspective, which we might call an "environmental" point of view.

The continuing explosive growth of computer technology is a self-fulfilling enterprise. Who will use the technology or how it will affect today's business organizations is not and cannot be the primary motivational factor in the discovery process. If we observe today's technologies and the organizations attempting to utilize them, we find a degree of incompatibility. This may be traceable in part to the fact that people and organizations change far more slowly than the technologies themselves. Let us examine this issue of incompatibility more closely by focusing first upon the specifics of the data processing organization and then more broadly upon the total business organization.

To some extent, what is technically possible tends to raise people's expectations regarding what ought to be accomplished. Thus, when the company vice-president reports on a conference he attended at which a prototype global database concept was demonstrated, the expectations of the data processing organization may be higher than before. When your chief programmer attends a seminar on data dictionary/directory technology, his expectations may rise to want to employ this newer technology in his next project. Thus, the data processing organization may find that as a result of people's expectations, it is continuously engaged in the experimental use of new technology without the proper organization or sufficient skill to ensure that the implementation will be anything but problematic.

An increasingly diverse computing technology has resulted in a second major impact on most data processing organizations — namely, increased specialization of its personnel. Whereas, in the past, an individual could be simultaneously a generalist and an expert (perhaps even for nearly the full range of available computer hardware and software), the expert today is more likely a specialist whose in-depth knowledge extends to a particular piece of software and a particular series of hardware. The significance of this increased requirement for technical specialization is that it has resulted in communications problems between technicians. Data processing has typically been organized as a single general-purpose entity within most businesses. Cohesiveness and cooperation within that organization was relatively easy to achieve in the early days of computing when the technology was less complex and diverse. Today, the systems programmer, database administrator, and applications programmer probably represent three conflicting viewpoints about what data processing is and how it ought to be applied.

The technological imperative has not limited its impact to simply the data processing organization. Rather, there appear to be important inconsistencies between the new technology and the manner in which most businesses organize themselves to do work. In particular, the evolution of database technologies has created a facility for development of computerized systems that cut across organizational lines of authority. Under the earlier technology, offices were expected to create and control "their" data files. Anyone seeking to modify or retrieve information contained in these files was supposed to go through the appropriate "owner" office. Thus, the data file was treated in much the same way as the old manual files. Essentially the same organizational structure used in the manual system was functional for the new computerized system.

In the database environment, many of these procedures change. For example, much of the data becomes elevated to the status of "institutional" data. Furthermore, for a sizable amount of the remaining data, the user office retains primary responsibility for only the transactional processing associated with it. Access to the data by others for purposes of inquiry, aggregation, and evaluation need not require prior office approval. The database technology supports a level of cross-organizational assessment by someone other than the originating offices.

Despite these dramatic new technical capabilities, one can observe relatively few changes in the way in which businesses are organized. The extent of incompatibility between cross-functional database technology and a business that is functionally organized will be evidenced in the degree of difficulty that organization will have in implementing the new technology.

The impact of technological innovations in real-time systems capabilities in conjunction with the previously mentioned database technology makes for additional incompatibilities with traditional organizations. Whereas previously an office could control the speed with which the actions of another office could affect it, this is clearly no longer the case. In an on-line, real-time environment, changes are immediate, as is the impact that the work of one office has on all others. The nature of the work performed, the control mechanisms required, and the kinds of problems experienced have all changed as a result of the technological innovation. An examination of the traditional organizational structure generally reveals that it has undergone minimal organizational change in anticipation of the new technology. Rather, it has left to chance the discovery of the kind of organizational structure that best supports the new technology. During the first few months of implementing the new technology, the organization may or may not discover its problem. If it does, it may be able to recover, albeit with great discomfort. If it does not, the new system will become the scapegoat and the old organization will persist.

Up to this point, we have concentrated only upon the unreadiness or inappropriateness of the organization relative to the new technology. To leave our discussion at this point would be unfair and unwise, for there is another side to the issue. Organizations are composed of complex and dynamic groupings of people. An organization's informational needs and requirements, as well as other factors associated with a computerized system, will change rapidly over time.

When we focus on very low-level systems (such as a payroll system), it is often possible to find similarities between the ways in which very different businesses operate. However, when we begin to explore the development of large-scale systems that integrate operational and managerial functions (for example, a financial management system), the differences between business organizations become pronounced.

These two factors — the dynamics and uniqueness of a business enterprise — are incompatible at times with the new technology. Recall that technology has evolved quite independently of how specific organizations work or what they need. While there has been considerable progress in resolving these problems, the fact remains that it takes time to develop individualized systems because it becomes necessary to precede actual development with an attempt at understanding particular organizational needs. Also, needed changes that require time and effort to accomplish will be made throughout the life of the system.

To some extent, data processing organizations have tended to "package" and/or "freeze" their products, since they recognize the time requirements of customization and change, and the lack of true flexibility in much of the technology itself. For large-scale systems development, we would be inclined to take an opposing point of view and side with some of the contingency-based comments about computer systems development: To develop effective systems, it is necessary to recognize that there is no one best way to construct a system; only a way that is best for a given situation.[10]

1.2.4 A growing thread of commonality

There are many ways of looking at an issue as complex as the problems associated with the development of large-scale, computerized information systems. The management, process, and technical/organizational incompatibility perspectives represent three increasingly popular points of view on the matter. They are particularly helpful since each, in its own way, seeks to identify specific problems for which some remedy can be constructed and implemented. Historically, we have, perhaps, overemphasized the differences between these perspectives and have even gone so far as to join one or another camp in the belief that it represents the truly correct position.

While there are differences between these perspectives in terms of the specific issues addressed, there is also great commonality at a global level. That is, they share in an increasingly prevalent concern for the individual and group interactions inherent in any large-scale systems development effort. To this extent, they each reflect the growing awareness that our understanding of how to use technology is generations behind our level of technological achievement. And, that progress in the application of technology will necessitate that we gain a greater understanding of the human and organizational interactions and environment that are implicit in the systems development process.

In recent years, a considerable body of literature on individual and/or organizational implications of systems development has begun to accumulate, but there is not, as yet, a sense of cohesiveness associated with it. The literature on teams and their use in systems development probably reflects the current level of understanding and the degree of cohesiveness that we generally find in the literature as a whole. For example, some of the writings on teams are specific in focusing on a single step in the systems development process such as computer programming, while others attempt a much broader scope. Some of the literature examines the interrelationship between technicians, while other refers to the relationships between technicians, managers, and the users of technology. Last, the writing on teams varies widely in quality, ranging from very superficial to very insightful. Notwithstanding its limitations, the literature has been instrumental in fostering significant changes — not the least of which has been an increasing willingness to experiment with new approaches to systems development.

1.3 Evidence of change

There is reason to believe that very rapid changes have already occurred and will continue to occur in the way in which systems are developed. The changes are evident, for example, when we explore how technicians work with one another; and also, when we examine the relationships between technician, manager, and user in the course of developing a new system. Naturally, the changes are not all to be found everywhere (or even in most places), but they can be observed with sufficient frequency to be impressive. In the following sections, we will examine each of these two situations.

1.3.1 Changes in how technicians work

Within the computing industry, the Golden Calf has long been technical expertise — plain and simple. The expert is an individual to whom many dollars and much deference are paid. This practice has served as a great motivational force in attracting and retaining bright and creative people and in encouraging these people to keep current with the rapidly changing technology. It has also served, in a less positive sense, as a protective veil for some questionable practices. For example, a lack of standardization and documentation has traditionally been tolerated, if not outright endorsed.

In his now classic book *The Psychology of Computer Programming,*[11] Weinberg popularized the notion of a need for greater openness between technicians, and pointed out that achieving this openness would require some dramatic changes in how the task of computer programming would be performed. He prophesized that the transitional process involved in asking computer programmers to write readable programs and in asking them to allow other programmers to read and pass judgment upon their code would be emotionally charged. It would not be a totally rational process of transition.

Notwithstanding considerable resistance to greater openness between technicians, the transition is underway and gaining momentum. Rather than continuing to shroud our problems in technical mystique, we are beginning to critically examine and evaluate how technicians work, pose interesting and creative solutions to traditional problems, and even quantify and measure the success or failure of a specific methodology. For example, recent use of peer ratings for judging the quality of computer programs[12] and the use of inspection teams[13] signify that the halcyon days of the technical guru may be rapidly coming to a close.

Until now, the examination of how technicians work together in the area of computer programming has been much sharper and far more extensive than research on how technicians work with non-technical personnel. Working with the programming process, Baker and Mills went beyond the level of concern for the individual alone and defined an innovative organizational structure known as the "chief programmer team."[14] Members of the team are assigned specific but complementary roles, so that checks and balances as well as backup are built into the team structure. The authors viewed this team approach as creating an environment that would serve to "move the programming production process from private art to public practice."*

Baker and Mills not only identified specific roles and functions within the team, but also sketched a process for creating multiple teams that could function with some degree of cohesiveness. Thus, in a relatively short time span, we have seen within the computer programming profession three levels of change being proposed and actively explored — the individual, group (or team), and intergroup levels.

1.3.2 Changes in management and user relationships

Unlike computer programming, the disciplines of systems analysis, design, and implementation involve both technical and non-technical people and issues. While the concepts and methods applied in exploring the working relationships between technicians are helpful, the environment in which the technician, manager, and user interact in these other systems areas is far more complex and dynamic.

Traditionally, the technician (systems analyst or systems designer) has been the dominant figure in this three-way relationship. What a system did and how it accomplished its work emanated from the systems person with only minimal and very general guidance and suggestion from others. Even the use of steering committees and the designation of specific users as EDP liaisons for their departments represented in many cases only the illusion of participation by others. To some extent, this was supported by the predominant view that technical issues such as computer hardware and software were the major obstacles to be overcome in developing effective computerized information systems.

Today, the predominant view is being challenged. Increasingly, greater participation by users and management is believed to be needed in systems development People problems, not technical problems, are the primary cause of disappointment and failure in the development of information systems.[15]

---

*F.T. Baker and H.D. Mills, "Chief Programmer Teams," *Datamation*, Vol. 19, No. 12 (December 1973), p. 58.

The question of who should be involved (and in what capacity) in the development of new systems is not easily answered. At this point, there appears to be a great deal of hit-or-miss activity in attempting to construct an environment within which a more balanced involvement between technician, manager, and user can occur. Observers of early team experiments have gained insight into some of the problems affecting the relationship. For example, systems personnel typically have difficulty in perceiving their design from the user's viewpoint, since they frequently do not understand the business process very well at all. On the other hand, the user typically lacks sufficient knowledge about computing to understand what is or is not feasible. Consequently, problems and misunderstandings are generally not apparent to either systems or user personnel until the moment of new system delivery — which is, of course, too late.[16]

To some extent, management and user personnel have simply become more vocal in challenging the traditional leadership role of the technician. Indeed, management and user communities in the past may have been *too* passive (or too befuddled), thereby allowing their concerns to remain somewhat peripheral. Now, however, such non-technical personnel are asserting, for example, that user department managers can and must provide the expertise needed to develop effective computerized systems.[17]

The technician's relationship to both management and user communities is in the early stages of a profound transition. Since a whole host of problems will need to be dealt with in the course of this transition, it will not happen quickly. Indeed, there is merit in a suggestion by O'Brien that what is required is a "user generation,"[18] and not another generation of computer hardware/software. As he has indicated, we are dealing with a wide variety of possible contributory causes to problems in these relationships. Simplistic, quick remedies do not generally work for complex problems.

In recent years, attempts have been made to apply team approaches in those stages of systems development where technician, manager, and user need to interact. These attempts were largely an outgrowth of the many reported success cases in the use of chief programmer teams. However, there are many obvious differences between the two environments and there is far greater complexity in the systems development arena than in the programming arena.

1.4 Summary

Despite the advanced technology and vast resources available, there remain numerous problems that affect our ability to develop effective computerized information systems in a timely fashion. Using a number of perspectives from which to view the problem, we can see that there are multiple deficiencies in how organizations currently attempt to implement a generally agreed-upon systems development strategy: First, the level of project management skill and the involvement of management personnel in the development process appears to be inadequate. Second, an overemphasis on formal versus informal business processes causes the resulting system to disagree with the way in which people, particularly managers, perform their work. This may result, in part, from a lack of communications skill and organizational awareness by many systems analysts and designers. And third, there appear to be very real incompatibilities between some of the new technology and the predominant organizational structures used by business. On the one hand, many organizations are still functionally organized (not very innovative), while database technology is more global (cross-functional/innovative). On the other hand, business has particular, dynamic needs, while technological products address general issues and are difficult to change (they remain static until the next software release).

All of these perspectives share a common focus upon individual and group interaction as being the crux of systems development problems. This has resulted in an increased interest in how to deal effectively with these problems and, as such, represents a deviation from the earlier contention that technical issues represented the primary obstacles to be dealt with in the development of effective new systems.

Changes in the ways in which technicians work with one another and with management and user communities are increasingly evident. Team approaches and other techniques that seek to make technicians more open with one another have gained popularity.

The establishment of an effective methodology that supports the technician, management, and user relationship is more difficult to achieve since the relationship is more complex. On balance, there is a move away from the technician's dominance of this relationship and, to some extent, a vying for power and control. The team approach, which is more fully discussed in the next chapter, is being aggressively explored as an alternative to deal with this relationship more effectively, and thus is being viewed as the potential key to developing more effective systems than have been possible to date.

Chapter 1: References

1. K.T. Orr, *Structured Systems Development* (New York: YOURDON Press, 1977), p. 3.

2. P.C. Semprevivo, *Systems Analysis* (Chicago: Science Research Assoc., 1976), pp. 1, 14–40.

3. S.P. Keider, "Why Projects Fail," *Datamation,* Vol. 20, No. 12 (December 1974), pp. 53–55.

4. J. Diebold, "Bad Decisions on Computer Use," *Harvard Business Review,* Vol. 47, No. 1 (January-February 1969), pp. 14–28, 176.

5. S.A. Huesing, "Team Approach and Computer Development," *Journal of Systems Management,* Vol. 28, No. 9 (September 1977), pp. 30–31.

6. L. Fried, "MIS Success Story: Smoothing out the People System," *Data Management,* Vol. 15, No. 7 (July 1977), pp. 30–36.

7. C. Argyris, "Management Information Systems: The Challenge to Rationality and Emotionality," *Management Services,* Vol. 17, No. 6 (February 1971), pp. 275–92.

8. C.F. Gibson and R.L. Nolan, "Managing the Four Stages of EDP Growth," *Harvard Business Review,* Vol. 52, No. 1 (January-February 1974), pp. 76–88.

9. P.C. Semprevivo, op. cit., pp. 2, 40–60.

10. S.A. Tomeski, "Building Human Factors into Computer Applications: The Computer Profession Must Overcome a 'Jackass Fallacy'!" *Management Datamatics,* August 1975, pp. 115–20.

11. G. Weinberg, *The Psychology of Computer Programming* (New York: Van Nostrand Reinhold, 1971).

12. N. Anderson and B. Shneiderman, "Use of Peer Ratings in Evaluating Computer Program Quality," *Proceedings of the Fifteenth Annual Computer Personnel Research Conference* (New York: Association for Computing Machinery, 1977), pp. 218–26.

13. T.D. Crossman, "Some Experiences in the Use of Inspection Teams," *Proceedings of the Fifteenth Annual Computer Personnel Research Conference,* op. cit., pp. 143–57.

14. F.T. Baker and H.D. Mills, "Chief Programmer Teams," *Datamation,* Vol. 19, No. 12 (December 1973), pp. 58—61. [Reprinted in E.N. Yourdon, ed., *Classics in Software Engineering* (New York: YOURDON Press, 1979), pp. 195—204.]

15. R.W. Holmes, "Twelve Areas to Investigate for Better MIS," *Financial Executive,* Vol. 38, No. 7 (July 1970), pp. 24—31.

16. C. Gane and T. Sarson, *Structured Systems Analysis: Tools and Techniques* (New York: Improved System Technologies, 1977), pp. 1—10.

17. E.M. Tolliver, "Myths of Automated Management," *Journal of Systems Management,* Vol. 22, No. 3 (March 1971), pp. 29—32.

18. J.A. O'Brien, "Overcoming Poor Performance by Coping with a User Generation," *Data Management,* Vol. 15, No. 6 (June 1977), pp. 38—42.

Systems Development Teams: Promise and Direction | 2

To be effective, a systems development team must become something more than a mere collection of individuals. As we shall see, characteristics such as cohesiveness, shared goals, and effective participation by all team members will differentiate the true team from the group that is a team in name only. Effective systems development teams will differ somewhat from programmer teams, planning and budgeting teams, or other kinds of teams. This is understandable since the environment, tasks, and participants involved in the process of systems development are unique to it.

In order to provide a firm basis for understanding current directions in the use of systems development teams and anticipated benefits for those organizations that successfully use those approaches, this chapter will briefly review relevant systems development problems evidenced in non-team and early team approaches; and closely examine current and future directions in the use of systems development teams.

With this chapter, we will have begun to describe, in general terms, some of the relevant characteristics of the systems development environment, tasks, and participants. We will also have begun to explore the relevance of the team approach for systems development and some of the expectations and promises associated with it by its advocates, thus building the frame of reference needed to direct a more in-depth search for information about teams and mechanisms for maximizing team effectiveness.

2.1 Relevant problems

Let's begin with some practical observations about systems departments and the way in which they have traditionally interacted with user departments. Observing the environment in which this interaction occurs reveals numerous problems that have typically reduced the effectiveness of that interaction, including

- differences in the prevailing rewards for systems and user personnel
- conflicting pressures regarding the application of current technology
- animosities resulting from the myth of technology's cost-reductive power

These problems and their impact on team and traditional approaches are explored in the section that follows. We'll also see in Section 2.1.2 how early experiments in the use of team approaches to systems development have been particularly instructive and have greatly influenced current directions in the use of systems development teams. Consequently, this brief review of some of the insights — and oversights — associated with early attempts at team development will provide substantiation for the current high degree of interest in topics such as team selection, team maintenance, and the physical work environment of teams.

2.1.1 Traditional non-team approaches

In most organizations, the unit (or units) charged with primary responsibility for systems development is either an integral part of the computing facility or has a special link to it. Thus, the systems department is most frequently organized separately from the various operational offices, such as accounting and personnel, with which it must work. Also, the department is associated either directly or indirectly with the computer as a technological unit.

The systems group is, of necessity, a very task-oriented group, whose success is largely measured by its ability to produce new products. In most business organizations, the systems department is given primary credit when systems development efforts are successful and primary blame when such efforts are unsuccessful.

A second observation about the prevailing systems development environment is that other operational units are generally rewarded on bases other than the extent to which they utilize current technology. In some instances, a user can obtain more reward by continuing to cope with an antiquated business methodology than it can by participating in a new systems development effort. Also, there appears to be little understanding by management regarding the workload that new systems development can have on the user who seeks to participate. Thus, in contrast to the perceptions of the systems department, we find that within the user department the following are true:

- The primary basis for reward is something other than using current technology.

- There may be more understanding and reward associated with not automating than with automating one's office.

- The workload associated with participating in new systems development will have to be absorbed on an overload basis.

Working in the field of computing is a commitment to work with an ever-changing, increasingly diverse technology. Thus, there is considerable professional pressure on systems personnel to continually upgrade their technical knowledge. This demand frequently conflicts with the pressure of the business organization to apply current (or not so current) skills and knowledge to development of functional, new systems. Therefore, from the systems professional's viewpoint, the pressures can be summarized as follows:

- There are professional pressures to be knowledgeable regarding state-of-the-art technology.

- There are organizational pressures to apply proved technology to business problems.

There are pressures as well to make a choice between the two since each is, in itself, an almost totally consuming set of demands on one's available time. As a closing observation about the environment in which systems departments operate, it should be mentioned that there remains today an expectation that computerized systems will minimally provide more service at the same cost and preferably reduce operating costs while improving service. The fact that computerization has not typically reduced costs dramatically appears to be a far less powerful influence than the myth, supported by management's pronounced expectations, that costs will decrease. This observation implies that at the very onset of systems development, the user department perceives the threat of diminished resources and associates that threat with the work of the systems department. Indeed, one can begin to observe, at the onset of a development project, a sort of adversarial relationship developing in which

- the systems department comes to be viewed as the instrument of technology

- the user department is threatened by the myths associated with the cost-reductive power of the technology
- the systems and user departments become hopelessly pitted against one another in a conflict that ostensibly has the full support of management

The traditional environment, as we've called it, has not been widely displaced, nor is it likely to be displaced in the immediate future. Therefore, the extent to which certain fundamental human and organizational problems and conflicts exist in the environment must be recognized. If the team approach is to be effective within this traditional environment, it must create a facility through which these and other important problems can be resolved. Obviously, any approach to systems development (teams included), if poorly executed, will simply aggravate an already problematic environment.

2.1.2 Observations about early teams

Early experiments in the use of team approaches to systems development have been instructive in telling us about team tasks and the team environment. However, they represent a very simplistic approach to a complex situation. Indeed, at times, they have been based on the naive assumption that somehow bringing a group of people together will result in a "team," and hence, greater productivity and better products. Using this unstructured hit-or-miss approach has created a track record for teams that is quite mixed — sometimes resulting in extraordinary success, sometimes in abysmal failure.

Observations about these early teams are important because they furnish us with facts about the team's success or failure and may provide guidelines for improvements in applying team approaches to future systems development efforts. The first observation to be noted is that systems development teams are almost universally "contrived." That is, teams do not form as a result of individuals' seeking out one another. Rather, the decision to develop a particular system results in the identification of prospective team members. Despite the fact that these teams are contrived, there do not appear to be any widely published and agreed-upon guidelines regarding criteria to be utilized in the selection of team members. Indeed, there is to some extent a visible conflict between systems, user, and management preferences. For example, the systems department, with its strong task orientation, would prefer those managers and users with knowledge and authority as participants. Since this would represent a major commitment of the most effective and critical members of those organizations, user and management groups frequently object.

While many of these team experiences represent sincere attempts at a new systems development strategy, they frequently do not take into account many important variables that can affect team performance. For example, the physical work environment and individual and group work styles, among other factors, all seem to be basically accepted as "givens." There also is little or no awareness of the extent to which these factors can significantly alter the performance of the team. This reflects, in part, an assumption that the concept of systems development teams is totally new and unique. In point of fact, there is a rich body of relevant research that can assist us in acquiring a more scientific understanding of those factors that influence team performance. Broadly categorized, the research literature being referenced falls into two areas:*

- the social psychology of small groups (of which teams can be considered a variant)

- organizational theory, analysis, and development

A final observation about early systems development teams is that they seemed to be almost exclusively task-oriented. Consequently, when teams experience problems such as interpersonal conflict with members of the team or with external individuals and groups, they are expected to muddle through somehow without losing momentum in doing the technical systems tasks. As stated earlier, a team is more than a collection of people. The true or ideal team is characterized by a sense of cohesiveness and common purpose. Yet, in our early application of team approaches, we seem to have overlooked the fact that at least some time needs to be spent on dealing with interpersonal problems. In a very pragmatic sense, an organization will not likely choose to postpone systems development for a prolonged period of time while it deals with team problems. At the same time, the legitimacy of attending to team problems must be recognized, and the skills needed to diagnose and deal with these sorts of problems should be built into the team organization.

2.2 Teams: current and future directions

It is clear from the discussions thus far that the major problems in developing computerized information systems extend far beyond the topics of effective computer hardware and software. Rather, human

---

*One of the objectives of Chapters 3 and 4 of this text is to describe those research findings that have particular relevance to team effectiveness.

and organizational issues like participation, communication, work style, and method of organization may be the primary culprits affecting success. Awareness of these issues has spurred the current interest in team approaches. What is unsettling is that one still does not find in the practice-based literature about systems development teams much attention to systematic thinking about how teams ought to be structured or how they ought to operate. Instead, one finds mostly vague speculations that getting the "right" people involved will somehow improve things. Moving toward the use of teams does not mean that we no longer have to worry about human and organizational problems. To the contrary, using the team approach places these factors center-stage in the systems development process. If the team approach is to be successful, we will need to utilize tools and techniques that facilitate team-member participation; gain a more realistic assessment of what teams can and cannot do; acquire a new set of skills associated with how individuals and groups interact in performing a job; and begin to build a base of research information to guide future application of team approaches.

2.2.1 Team-member participation

Several factors complicate the issue of participation for members of systems development teams: First, most large-scale information systems will affect several levels of an organization's hierarchy, including people performing the day-to-day work, their supervisors, middle managers, and top management. This implies that more than one organizational level should be involved in development of such large-scale systems.[1] Second, the proposed information system probably will cut across the functional organization. Thus, we might expect that purchasing, accounting, budgeting, and other departments will be affected by a new financial information system. If team participation is to reflect the involvement of people from throughout the organization in order for everyone to contribute a special brand of knowledge and ability to the team, then it will be necessary to structure individual involvement so that it is constructive and meaningful; that is, each will need a specific role to play.[2]

The third factor that complicates the issue of team-member participation has been set forth clearly by Brooks.[3] He points out that designing a large-scale system requires efficiency and conceptual integrity, qualities that are best supplied by a few good minds. A dilemma is created, however, since the effort of many people is required to complete large, complex tasks in an acceptable time-frame.

Finally, there is a potential negative relationship between broad participation and a tendency toward over-design. Opening the design process to the many diverse quarters of an organization entails a very real risk that the process might become an attempt to accomplish everything for everyone. The result could be an unwieldy design, exceeding the capabilities of the resources available to implement it. In describing what he calls the "second-system effect," Brooks warns that the tendency toward over-design is particularly great after a first successful system has been implemented.[4]

2.2.2 Promise of greater team productivity

Reports on the use of teams in systems development indicate that teams may have performance advantages over individual approaches. For example, if properly utilized, teams will be synergistic in the sense of achieving beyond what would be expected by the team members individually.[5] Shaw developed the following hypotheses about group versus individual performance:

- The mere presence of others increases the motivation level of a performing individual.

- Group judgments are superior to individual judgments for tasks that involve random error.

- Groups usually produce more and better solutions to problems than do individuals working alone.

- Groups learn faster than individuals.

- More new and radical ideas are produced by both individuals and groups when critical evaluation of ideas is suspended during the production period.

- Decisions made after group discussion are more risky than decisions made by the average individual prior to group discussion.[6]

Shaw's conclusions are most encouraging; however, some caution is needed in making the leap from the laboratory study of small groups to assumptions about synergistic teams. There is no guarantee that judgments about systems design, for example, involve random error, or that "more time" as it is defined for small tasks might not be an "unacceptable delay" in developing a new system. Nor is there complete agreement on this issue. For example, Harrison concludes that the group decision-making ability is frequently better than that of the average individual, but seldom better than that of the best individual, and that the group's superior performance may be attributable to the efforts of one superior decision-maker on the team.[7]

Notwithstanding differences on the matter, some important conclusions may be gleaned from the research. There is good reason to expect that team approaches to systems development will result in more alternative, and more innovative, solutions in a problem-solving environment; and, ultimately, in the development of better solutions on the average, provided that proper individuals have been selected. However, working to quick solutions is not a characteristic of group behavior. Thus, for systems development teams, we should expect greater productivity to mean more creative and qualitatively superior products. The tradeoff is that the team in all likelihood will take more time to accomplish its task.*

2.2.3 Learning about teams

Many factors can significantly influence the effectiveness with which a team performs its work. To isolate the specific factors that relate to systems development teams, we need to learn about the team as a dynamic organizational entity; learn what can be done to maximize team effectiveness; and learn to diagnose and evaluate team performance, and to initiate corrective action.

These topics are quite different from those addressed in most current textbooks on systems development. Thus, there is a degree of novelty that will necessitate a somewhat different, non-traditional mind-set about what is important to effective systems development. The decision to utilize the team approach ought to carry with it another implicit decision — namely, a focus upon the dynamics of team behavior, since therein lies the potential for ultimate success or failure.

However, it simply is not possible to capture the full essence of team dynamics only through reading. In particular, learning to diagnose and evaluate team performance, and to initiate corrective action when problems exist, will require the development of specific skills through application of concepts. Suffice it to say at this point that this represents a third important area in learning about teams.

---

*At this point, remember that there are some important differences between a true team and a group of individuals: The positive attributes cited above are potentially beneficial results of team performance. If the team were a cohesive, well-functioning entity, composed of very bright and capable individuals, then we would expect the quality of work to be greater than if the team were composed of bright and capable individuals in a state of continuous conflict. Also, while teams do take more time than individuals to perform tasks, there are huge differences in the amount of time that different teams require. Again, this is related to the overall effectiveness with which the team is able to work. This topic is treated in the next section.

2.2.4 The need for research

Much of the relevant research on teams is not found in the systems development literature. Rather, those disciplines dealing with the social psychology of small groups and organizational theory and analysis represent the primary repositories for the information we require. One of the problems in attempting to use that information is that many of these research studies are performed in a laboratory environment, and on groups whose objectives are less structured and task-oriented than those confronting a systems development team.* Such are the limitations of the available information. Yet, on balance, it provides us with a more scientifically based starting point than we have attempted to use thus far in the short history of systems development teams.

There is obviously a great need for "action research," to examine team approaches to systems development amid the complexities of the real world. Because it is impossible to hold constant all of the variables affecting team and individual performance, this form of research probably will yield results that are somewhat "softer" and less conclusive than those available from the laboratory. This should not dissuade us, but rather encourage us to proceed now with a form of research on systems development teams for which there is little precedent but potentially great value.

A final point on this matter of research has to deal with measurement: Action research has tended to be more subjective and judgmental than probably necessary. Thus, we hear about "greater productivity," "less resistance," and similar sorts of results that might have been, but were not, quantified by the observer. Recognizing the difficulties of quantifying results, researchers must nevertheless make a further attempt at direct, quantifiable measurement.

2.3 Summary

Traditional approaches to systems development have frequently created an environment that was not supportive of a positive relationship between systems, management, and user personnel. For example, most of the rewards or blame for new systems development were given to the systems development organization, while the reward structure for users and managers frequently encouraged non-participation and sticking with the old system. Second, demands on the systems professional

---

*A possible exception is the research belonging to the field of organization development, which applies relevant social and behavioral theory to its findings while maintaining a pragmatic process orientation.

from the data processing profession to remain current and demands from the business organization to use proved technology were frequently in direct competition with each other. Finally, management's insistence that computerization should equate with cost reduction frequently generated an adversarial relationship between systems and user personnel.

Early experiments in the use of the team approach to systems development tended to view the process in an oversimplified way. To some extent, they proceeded on the naive assumption that designating a group of people as a team was sufficient to ensure greater productivity and better results. These early efforts made very little reference to the literature on small-group behavior and organizational theory, and thus overlooked important variables that affect team effectiveness and that can be manipulated to improve team performance.

Future directions in the use of systems development teams will increasingly focus upon human and organizational issues, including the development and use of tools and techniques that facilitate team-member participation. Selecting the right people, giving them a meaningful role, and creating an environment in which they can succeed in the development of a large-scale system are complicated issues that must be effectively resolved.

Despite the problems, a number of potential benefits are to be accrued from the team approach that, on balance, make it desirable. Specifically, more numerous, creative, and better solutions are attributable to the team, versus the individual, approach. However, time required to obtain a solution will also be greater for the team.

Learning about teams involves three areas of concern: considering teams as a dynamic organizational entity; maximizing team effectiveness; and diagnosing and evaluating team performance and initiating corrective action. In the remainder of Part I, we will directly address the first two items listed. The third will be treated in Part II. This learning process can be facilitated by a combination of reading about teams and practicing in the analysis and evaluation of team behavior. Guidance in learning how to apply these concepts skillfully is the primary agenda for Part II of this book.

Finally, researchers should develop and use more quantified methods of measurement. Several such techniques to achieve greater quantification are presented in Chapter 4.

Chapter 2: References

1.   G.W. Dickson, "Management Info-Decision Systems," *Business Horizons,* Vol. 11, No. 6 (December 1968), pp. 17-26.

2.   D. Katch, "Bridging the MIS Gap," *Infosystems,* Vol. 25, No. 7 (July 1978), pp. 58–60.

3.   F.P. Brooks, Jr., *The Mythical Man-Month* (Reading, Mass.: Addison-Wesley, 1975).

4.   Ibid., pp. 51–58.

5.   K.M. Bartol, "Building Synergistic Teams," *Proceedings of the Fifteenth Annual Computer Personnel Research Conference* (New York: Association for Computing Machinery, 1977), pp. 18–30.

6.   M.E. Shaw, *Group Dynamics* (New York: McGraw-Hill, 1976), pp. 3, 78–80.

7.   E.F. Harrison, *The Managerial Decision-Making Process* (Boston: Houghton-Mifflin, 1975), p. 210.

Learning More About Teams | 3

In working with systems development teams, we must recognize that team interaction produces significant results at three primary levels:

- results specific to the individual team member

- those specific to team operation and behavior

- results affecting the team's relationship to the rest of the organization[1]

The quality of team interaction will determine, in large part, the effectiveness with which it will function at each of these levels, and thereby determine the degree of success in developing a useful new system. Effective team interaction can have positive results for the individual, such as increased motivation to work on the development project, increased sense of belonging to the group, and improved self-image. It can also create a structure and environment that will facilitate the setting of team goals, job assignments, decision-making, and team cohesiveness, and have other positive team-level results. Finally, effective team interaction can result in improvements to the overall organization by stimulating improved communications both vertically and laterally throughout the organization.

In this chapter, we will begin to develop a description of the team as an organizational entity, and identify several possible variations on the concept of team structure. Also, we will explore the issue of when to use teams, and provide a conceptual framework that underscores their dynamic character. Finally, we will briefly highlight the team activities that are most critical in assuring overall team effectiveness and those that are most susceptible to problems.

3.1 Teams and task forces

The terms "task force" and "team" are sometimes used interchangeably. At other times, their meanings appear to have different emphases, as in the use of task forces to mean advisory groups that develop recommendations, while teams refer to work groups that develop functional products. Galbraith has differentiated the two, not upon the basis of function or purpose, but rather upon their duration as an organizational entity.[2] That is, task forces are temporary group structures designed to deal with problems or projects of short duration, while teams are more or less permanent group structures. Because large-scale systems development efforts can extend over a period of years, and because the group member association may be expected to continue long after completion of the actual systems component, we have opted to use the term team, as opposed to task force, throughout this text. In so doing, we will avoid the possible misconception of the systems development team as an advisory group that makes recommendations. To the contrary, it must be a work group responsible for effective development of a new system.

3.2 Organizational objectives

Developing a large-scale information system necessitates that informational requirements be established both vertically (at different management levels) and laterally (across functional lines of the organization). This process requires that the developers of the system make thousands of individual decisions about how the system will function. If each issue requiring a decision had to go up and down the bureaucratic hierarchy for resolution, those communication channels would soon be overloaded, the delays would be excessive, and in all probability the development would never be completed. Alternatively, if the decisions were resolved without effective vertical and lateral communications, the design, although completed, might be rejected as not reflecting the needs and expectations of others.

The team concept seeks to establish an organizational structure that will facilitate lateral forms of communication and joint decision-making, rather than simply refer problems higher in the hierarchy for resolution, and to establish one that can be further integrated within the organization or linked to higher levels of management. The first of these objectives (lateral integration) is practically accomplished by having as team members those representing the various functional areas affected by the new system.

The second objective (vertical integration) is usually accomplished in one of two ways. First, the team may be structured so that one top-level manager acts as coordinator. Alternatively, a management representative may join the team. However, there are other options to formally structure the team in a way that facilitates both lateral and vertical integration. These options are not widely used at this time, because they place greater autonomy and decision-making authority within the team — a bold step that transfers power from functional management. Nevertheless, they are worthy of limited attention and are therefore discussed briefly in the next section.

3.2.1 Extensions of the team concept

Because of the team's diverse membership, there are times when leadership, coordination, and control problems may affect team performance. Again Galbraith has provided several organizational design alternatives that could be used in tandem with the team approach.[3] For example, when leadership of the team becomes a problem, the organization may opt to create a new role with the power, influence, and leadership skill needed to convert a contrived collection of individuals into an effective team. This role is referred to as either an "integrating" or a "managerial linking" role, depending upon whether its purpose is facilitation of the team's decision-making process (integration), or direct participation in the decision-making process, approval authority, and budgetary control (management link). In neither case does the team formally report to the person in this new position.

Indeed, for most systems/user/management teams in operation today, team members do not report to the team leader in any formal sense. To the contrary, they continue to report formally within their functional area. Furthermore, the team leader is only infrequently a specially selected individual responsible for integration, and very rarely an individual with decision-making authority and budgetary control of the project. However, as more and more experience continues to accrue in the use of systems development teams, one can expect to find an increasing number of direct attempts at utilizing these extensions to the team approach.

A somewhat different alternative is commonly referred to as the "matrix organization," which introduces the notion of dual reporting relationships in addition to preserving many of the integrating components mentioned above. For example, a member of a systems development team that is part of a matrix organization formally reports to both a functional manager and the team project manager. Hence, evaluations of the team member's performance are made by both managers.

The intent of the matrix organization is to create a power balance between the functional department and the team, which may have different objectives and priorities. Again, matrix approaches are not widely used in conjunction with systems development teams at this time, because they require an undesirable transfer of power and autonomy to the team. However, the matrix approach does represent one possible future direction in the continuing evolution of systems development team concepts and practices.

3.3 When to use teams

The problems associated with large-scale systems design and the potential benefits of team approaches have served to heighten our enthusiasm for the use of systems development teams. While a lack of understanding and faulty execution of the team approach may represent the primary reasons for the failure of some early attempts at team development, there may be conditions under which it is not advisable to use a team approach to systems development.

Stating the matter in a positive way, Hackman has indicated that a group-based work design seems warranted when one or more of the following conditions is present:

1. The product is such that individual work is not realistically possible.

2. The technology or physical work-setting is such that high interdependence of workers is required.

3. Individuals have high social needs that could be capitalized upon through group work.

4. Group work would considerably raise the overall motivating potential of the employee's job.[4]

Using the above criteria, we can establish some guidelines for deciding when to use team approaches. First, as we have previously noted, when the systems development project is large and complex, it is not realistic to expect that a single individual will have sufficient knowledge and skill to perform all aspects of the work in an acceptable time-frame. Under such conditions, the team approach would appear warranted. However, the converse of this is also true: If the nature of the project is such that a single individual could complete the product in an acceptable time-frame, we would unnecessarily restrict use of that individual as a valuable resource by blindly insisting that he or she obtain a group consensus on each and every aspect of the work.

In determining the size of a team, we should also consider this point — namely, that real work requirements and not conventions should be used to determine the size of the development team. The purpose of team approaches is not to replace individualism with group action, but rather to apply both individual and group approaches in the environments to which they are appropriate.

The second criterion listed above is open to interpretation. For example, is computer programming a type of work (technology) that requires high interdependence? Traditionally, it has been treated as though only minimal coordination with others was required for a programmer to perform effectively. Advocates of team approaches to programming have argued differently, emphasizing that programs are effective only when they are readable by others who will have to maintain them, and when they adhere to pre-established standards; and that the attainment of this goal is only insured through a high degree of interaction during development of the program. The actual amount of interaction required is probably a function of the clarity of programming standards and conventions. For example, as organizations begin to apply such techniques as structured walkthroughs, organization members may find the time spent on interaction decreasing as a function of people's working in concert with similar expectations.

In the design of a new system, the degree of clarity about what is required from the new system may be significant in determining whether a team approach is needed. With a great deal of clarity, the team approach may not be warranted. Rather, an individual approach may be used, providing those affected by the project are given the opportunity to review and evaluate results. Conversely, when the systems requirements are not clearly understood a priori, the team approach that maximizes the opportunities for interaction appears preferable.

Data processing professionals have traditionally been typified as individualistic people with little need or desire to engage in highly social work activities. It is always difficult to determine whether people behave as they do in order to express their inner selves, or because they try to meet the expectations of others whose opinions "count." Without being overly philosophical about the matter, we can suggest that data processing professionals have been stereotyped, and that there are talented people who do have high social needs, which could be capitalized upon through group work. Viewing the desire to engage in group work as an acceptable alternative and not as a sign of technical weakness is an important first step. However, it must also be remembered that establishing the legitimacy of social need does not mean that everyone will want to engage in team work. To insist blindly that all individuals need to work with others will be a disservice to some individuals, and thus to the larger organization.

The fourth item mentioned by Hackman (motivating the employee) is not unrelated to its immediate predecessor in the sense that meeting social needs can be a rewarding and, hence, motivating factor. However, this criterion does strike more broadly at the issue of rewards. The opportunities to obtain greater visibility, to be associated with others held in high esteem, and to work in an environment in which peer-group rewards and recognition are obtainable on an almost daily basis can be highly motivating. When staff members agree that these factors are important to them, these shared perceptions strongly suggest the use of a team approach. Also, when large numbers of new staff are introduced into an organization, the use of a team approach may be an opportunity to capitalize upon this limited but important point of commonality. Conversely, when employees' perceptions of the project are negative, insistence upon the team approach could actually reduce, rather than increase, individual motivating potential.

Certainly, if none of the above conditions are present, the team approach should be avoided; if all conditions are present, then only the team approach should be considered. However, as with most issues, reality seems to exist somewhere in the large gray area between the two absolutes. The problem is complicated by qualitative as well as quantitative factors. For example, there may be such an intense sense of the importance of individual prerogatives that it would be unwise to proceed with a team approach, despite the presence of other conditions that would appear to support use of the team approach. In any event, our purpose here has been to present the most critical factors influencing a decision regarding the use of teams. Each situation is unique and hence requires the best professional judgment of the decision-maker based upon these criteria.

3.4 Team dynamics

Enlisting a group of people to work together for the first time to perform some important but loosely understood activity, such as design of a new system, creates an environment in which the level of interpersonal dynamics may indeed produce wide-ranging results: The results may vary from highly positive to very dysfunctional. In addition, they may not be consistent for all aspects of the work. For example, in designing a large-scale personnel system, team members may agree on the matter of data requirements, but strongly disagree about who should be permitted access to that data.

To gain further insight into effective team performance, we need to examine the dynamics of team activity from two perspectives. The first of these perspectives examines the dynamic process whereby the group evolves from a contrived collection of individuals to a cohesive team. Tuckman has identified four stages in this dynamic process:

- forming — the group begins to identify with its common task and creates a team structure believed to facilitate achievement of its goals

- storming — the proposed structure becomes unacceptable to the individual team members as they perform the tasks and recognize the extent of compromise necessary

- norming — the group restructures itself — this time with team norms (formal and informal rules and expectations) and with more openness and greater acceptance of others

- performing — the group becomes a problem-solving entity without the need to divert energy and resources to resolution of interpersonal problems[5]

Naturally, a team may be at different evolutionary stages for different issues. Nor is the process strictly linear, since problems experienced on one issue can undermine prior progress made with other issues. Nonetheless, Tuckman's typology is valuable in bringing to the fore the realization that teams are an evolving, dynamic entity. The particular kinds of problems teams confront depend partly upon the stage of their development. Also, the type of assistance that might be of value to the team could be expected to vary from one stage to another. For example, if a team is experiencing difficulty in acquiring a consensus regarding its purpose (forming stage), it would be inappropriate to treat it as if it were a cohesive problem-solving entity (performing stage), capable of solving internal problems without external assistance. As obvious as this appears within the context of Tuckman's work, it is frequently ignored in real-life assessments of systems development team performance.

A second perspective about team dynamics, which complements the evolutionary perspective, has previously been mentioned. Lawrence and Lorsh have set forth a perspective commonly referred to as "contingency theory."[6] Stated simply, contingency theory proposes that there is no one best way to design or change an organization. Rather, the focus should be on selecting a design or change strategy in a manner that assures a proper "fit" between the organization and its environment. This theory supports our prior statements about teams as one alternative approach to systems development, not as a panacea to be blindly applied in all situations.

However, the contingency theory also provides an opportunity for understanding more fully the complexity of interpersonal dynamics within the team itself. For example, applying the theory raises questions such as, What kind of team leadership style would be most effective for a systems development team in the storming stage versus one in the performing stage? or, What kind of team organization (for example, bureaucratic or matrix) would be more appropriate if the tasks were predictable (program coding) versus unpredictable (systems analysis)? The use of this approach does not enable us to make broad generalizations from which to develop uniform strategies, but therein lies its usefulness: It forces us to assess the problem fully before arriving at conclusions and developing prescriptions.

3.5 Team problems and effectiveness

In attempting to perform as an effective work group, the team may encounter any or all of three major types of problems that have been summarized by Huse as follows:

- problems relating to the tasks and activities that the group must perform

- problems relating to the processes by which the group performs its task

- problems relating to interpersonal conflict[7]

Typically, in systems development work, we have overemphasized the importance of the first type of problem. Thus, we have sought to assess many problems as if they were technological problems — that is, we assume that delays in the delivery of a new system reflect a lack of technical or managerial expertise. Alternatively, we could consider the possibility that problems in group process or interpersonal conflict, not task-related expertise, might be at fault. In point of fact, these latter problems frequently are the major ones. Consequently, much of the remainder of this book will focus on strategies for analyzing and evaluating process and interpersonal problems, as well as strategies for resolving these non task-related problems.

Focusing more directly upon process and interpersonal issues, Schein has identified six major areas of group concern that must be reasonably addressed if effective performance is to be achieved:

- interpersonal communications within the group
- member roles and functions within the group
- group problem-solving and decision-making processes
- group norm development and individual growth opportunities
- group leadership and authority relationships
- intergroup cooperation and competition[8]

A more detailed description of each area and Schein's contributions will be presented in Chapter 4 under the topic of process consultation. Suffice it to say at this point that the systems profession has not traditionally addressed these important issues in any great depth. Consequently, in the ensuing discussions, we will frequently turn to research literature in other disciplines for support and direction, most notably in the field of organization development.

The next chapter presents practical suggestions that can be readily applied to improve overall team effectiveness. The latter portions of the chapter briefly describe frequently used organization development (OD) strategies that necessitate the involvement of a highly trained OD practitioner to be effective. The descriptions are included simply to increase the reader's general understanding about the nature and variety of services available from professional OD consultants.

3.6 Summary

The quality of team interaction will affect the team at the individual, group, and intergroup levels. Individual satisfaction, team-member cooperation, and effectiveness in dealing with external groups can facilitate successful development of a new system.

The team structure is designed to encourage lateral forms of communication, and can be extended to provide essential vertical linkage between the team and upper echelons of management.

As additional experience is gained in the use of team approaches in systems development, extensions will probably be made to the basic team model to include integrating role, managerial linking role, and even matrix organization concepts.

The decision to use a team approach should be based upon a prudent evaluation of existing conditions that support and/or argue against team approaches. A decision to utilize a team approach appears to be supported if the product is such that individual work is not realistically possible; the technology or physical work requires high worker interdependence; individuals have social needs that could be capitalized upon through group work; and if group work would considerably raise the overall motivating potential of the employee's job.

Insight into effective team performance is enhanced by an understanding of both the evolutionary development of the team and of the importance of viewing the team from a contingency perspective. Through these two perspectives, the dynamic nature of the team becomes more apparent, and decisions and actions regarding it become more respectful of its true complexity.

There has been a tendency to misdiagnose team problems as being task-related. Consequently, this text will continually emphasize, where appropriate, problems related to group process and interpersonal conflict as well as those related to tasks.

Chapter 3: References

1. E.F. Huse, *Organization Development and Change* (St. Paul, Minn.: West Publishing, 1975), pp. 230−32.

2. J.R. Galbraith, *Organization Design* (Reading, Mass.: Addison-Wesley, 1977), pp. 8, 111−27.

3. Ibid., pp. 10, 148−66.

4. J.R. Hackman, "Work Design," *Improving Life at Work,* eds. J.R. Hackman and J.L. Suttle (Santa Monica, Calif.: Goodyear Publishing, 1977), pp. 96−162.

5. B.W. Tuckman, "Developmental Sequence in Small Groups," *Psychological Bulletin,* Vol. 63, No. 6 (1965), pp. 384−99.

6. P. Lawrence and J. Lorsh, *Developing Organizations: Diagnosis and Action* (Reading, Mass.: Addison-Wesley, 1969), pp. 60−83.

7. E.F. Huse, op. cit., p. 48.

8. E.H. Schein, *Process Consultation: Its Role in Organization Development* (Reading, Mass.: Addison-Wesley, 1969), p. 13.

Maximizing Team Effectiveness | 4

In this chapter, we will explore some of the suggestions and professional strategies for maximizing team effectiveness. For those who are planning to begin a team development effort, the chapter should provide valuable assistance in the planning process and should facilitate anticipating the sorts of problems and issues that arise in the course of team development. For those who are already immersed in the team development process and experiencing problems, the chapter should provide insight into those problems, some practical suggestions for self-improvement, and direction in selecting and acquiring the kinds of external assistance that may be required.

The chapter is divided into three basic components: First, practical suggestions that can be directly applied by the reader are presented. Second, a rather extensive section is included on decision-making processes, since this is an area in which many teams experience numerous problems. Last, frequently used organization development strategies are described to further emphasize the extent to which organizational issues, as well as technical issues, are central to the success of a systems development team effort.

4.1 Practical suggestions for improving team performance

Traditionally, systems personnel have been trained to work independently, both in one-on-one situations and in more formal situations, for example, when they must speak before a group. Consequently, it is not surprising that they sometimes have problems in adjusting to the team environment, in which group sessions known as team meetings are the primary vehicle for doing the work.

There are a number of readily employed tools and techniques that can improve the effectiveness with which a team operates in these meetings or work sessions. For example, based upon my own observations of four systems development teams, I suggest the following techniques to improve the effectiveness of the team meeting:

1. When possible, schedule the team meetings early (even before the work day!).

2. Do not schedule the meeting unless everyone can attend.

3. Do not start the meeting until everyone is present.

4. Cancel the meeting after twenty minutes if attendance is incomplete.

5. Prepare a detailed agenda for each meeting.

6. Actively solicit criticism and comment from all team members for each item.

7. Encourage development of tangible products (however tentative), as opposed to simply discussing what must be done.

8. Complete one agenda item before going on to the next.

9. Be sure that each person leaves the meeting with something to do for the next meeting, either individually or with others.

10. Publish daily minutes that highlight agreed-upon items.[1]

Fordyce and Weil suggest five methods that result in better group meetings:[2] First, using large sheets of paper or chart pads to display significant points enables participants to grasp what is really going on in the meeting, helps maintain discipline, imparts a sense of direction, prevents important items from being lost, and provides a useful form of documentation.

Second, asking each person in the room, in sequence, to state his or her position is suggested as a method of assuring the participation of all team members. Fordyce and Weil believe that this practice avoids domination of the meeting by a few and also serves as an excellent way of summarizing a meeting, providing there is a reasonable level of trust between team members.

Third, Fordyce and Weil suggest critiquing (either planned or spontaneous) as a method for periodically measuring the effectiveness of an activity. Individual critiques must be kept simple and direct, since they are intended as a way for each person to give precise feedback to the team, which can then use the feedback to improve team effectiveness. Care must be taken not to permit people to misuse the technique, employing it as a platform from which to vocalize general discontent.

Dividing the team into subgroups of two or more can be useful in collecting needed information, in working on specific items that do not require the full resources of the team, or as a way of making progress when the full-team approach is getting bogged down.

Fordyce and Weil's final suggestion focuses upon meetings between the team and external groups, such as lower-level management. To hold these meetings, they suggest using the fishbowl method, in which the invited participants and team members arrange themselves in concentric circles or semicircles (as illustrated in Fig. 4.1). This approach stimulates a more spontaneous interchange between the team and other groups.

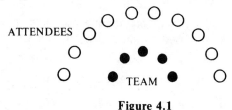

Figure 4.1

The fishbowl technique should not be used as an alternative to formal presentations in which it is important for the speaker to have full control over the delivery of information to an audience that is there primarily to listen. However, the technique is suggested as a way of stimulating a more spontaneous interchange between the team and other groups that have a direct interest in the systems development project.

The opportunities for successful application of the above practical suggestions will be greatly enhanced if the team members themselves possess strong interpersonal communications skills. Listening, watching, questioning, interviewing, and issuing survey questionnaires are skills that must be developed within the team membership. A six-stage educational training program has been developed for systems analysts, and it could be practically extended to meet the needs of the systems development team. The program includes

- an orientation that seeks to sensitize the group to the importance of effective interpersonal communications

- formal training in interpersonal communications theory and application

- learning in a controlled environment through the use of role-playing and case study approaches
- on-the-job training wherein an experienced person accompanies the novice as a silent partner and provides critiques afterward
- self-awareness sessions, in which the individual discusses with others his or her feelings and attitudes and their impact on work performance
- periodic seminars that introduce new ideas and approaches[3]

While an organization's budget will determine the extent to which such a program can be formalized, it should not be difficult to divert at least some resources to this effort, much as programmer training and training in specific applications have managed to acquire resource support.

4.2 Effective team decision-making

During the course of its existence, the systems development team will need to make many decisions, ranging from major, global design decisions to relatively minor decisions, such as those concerning standard data names. It is, therefore, important for the team to employ decision-making processes that are reliable, effective, and efficient. In so doing, it will be possible to avoid situations in which the entire team engages in a multi-day discussion about suitable data names, or decides within fifteen minutes that a total MIS approach is the only proper approach. In this section, we outline a process to be followed in making significant systems decisions that involve most or all team members. There are three stages in making a decision:

1. data collection
2. data aggregation and presentation
3. reaching a decision

Since each stage is important, the temptation to jump quickly to step 3 should be avoided. Each stage is described in the following sections.

4.2.1 Data collection

Selecting a data collection tool relates to the kind of information to be collected. For example, do we need to collect new ideas, or opinions about data already collected? Are we looking for ideal solutions, or solutions that are politically acceptable? There are many useful techniques that can be used to collect data, and six of them are briefly explained below:

Estimate — This is a quick and useful technique for very simple situations in which a great deal of information is already known. For example, when all of the team members have a list of the items to be considered for inclusion in a systems package, ask the team members to provide a point estimate or a range estimate* for those items.

Talk/estimate — In situations in which there is less generally known data, it is advisable first to exchange information and then move into the estimate stage.

Estimate/talk/estimate — Since members of systems development teams frequently have very different backgrounds and perspectives, it is sometimes useful for them to present their opinions (estimate), discuss all of the opinions presented (talk), and re-express their opinions on the basis of their new information (estimate).

Nominal group process — At times, the team's goal is to obtain many ideas quickly. For example, let us imagine that our team needs to make a formal presentation to top management. There will be time constraints on the presentation, and many topics to be covered in the small amount of time. Using the nominal approach, we would ask each team member to jot down the five most critical topics to be covered in the presentation. The second stage in the process would be to construct a single list of all topics and indicate the frequency of their occurrence. The process is particularly beneficial in that it focuses participants' efforts on a specific task, enables all members to contribute, and eliminates the possibility of using the team meeting to exchange adversarial niceties on irrelevant topics.

Brainstorming — In many ways, this is simply a vocal version of the nominal group process. However, because it is a vocal process, two rules must be strictly enforced in dealing with the suggestions made by the team members. First, someone acts as a reporter to record ideas exactly as they are

---

*One type of point estimate is to rate an option on a scale of one to ten. A type of range estimate is to describe something as good to very good, for example, or, in numerals, from five to seven on a ten-point scale.

stated. Second, and more important, no evaluation of the ideas expressed is permitted. If someone indicates that he does not agree with an idea, he is simply advised of the opportunity for discussion at the end of the meeting. The high degree of interaction involved in brainstorming can result in generating many creative ideas, but can suffer if less vocal people do not participate, or if the task leader does not keep participants on the proper track.

Synthetic groups — Techniques to collect data from an identifiable group of people without actually bringing them together as a group include interviews, surveys, or the Delphi technique (utilization of known experts on the subject). By obtaining the information individually, we avoid position battles and interpersonal conflict; and we can minimize threat by keeping responses anonymous. These techniques can be particularly useful to the team in dealing with external individuals and groups.

To collect data about an issue or problem, one or a combination of the above techniques should be utilized. Furthermore, as the team works on different issues, it is best to vary the technique that is employed. To overuse a single technique robs the team of the opportunity for variety in its work.

4.2.2 Data aggregation and presentation

Once data collection is completed, it is important to aggregate and present the data prior to actual decision-making. This is probably the most frequently overlooked step in the decision-making process, and therefore can be considered the most crucial area for improving decision-making.

In order to select a proper technique, we must establish the criteria by which data will be aggregated. For example, if we are evaluating several systems design alternatives, will we rank each of them on the basis of low cost, ease of use, positive public relations, or multiple attributes? Proper data aggregation relates to the intended use of the data: In particular, we will need to establish whether we are looking for comparisons, predictions, or estimations of magnitude. Techniques for data aggregation are described on the next pages for each of these three categories.

1. *Comparisons* — The following techniques may be used to aggregate data for comparative purposes:

   ☐ Voting — Have each team member choose one alternative. The technique is quick, easy, and overused, and gives little information about interrelationships and relative differences.

   ☐ Equivalence grouping — Have team members divide a set of items into two piles, one of which is more important than the other. This technique is sometimes used in conjunction with ranking.

   ☐ Ranking — Have members rank all items highest to lowest to get a better sense of "order of difference," which is not obtained by voting. Using ranking in conjunction with equivalence grouping increases efficiency, since it reduces time spent on items of little importance. Ranking is sometimes referred to as the Q-sort technique.

   ☐ Rating — Ask each team member to rate each alternative on a scale of one to ten. The technique provides a better sense of the relative weight between alternatives. For example, the number one choice may be a ten, while the number two choice is a seven and the number three choice is a six.

   ☐ Paired comparison — Have the members compare each alternative to all others, one at a time, for each criterion (for example, low cost or ease of use). This can be a time-consuming process, and should be employed only for major decisions.

2. *Predictions* — At times, it is important to aggregate and present data with an eye toward predicting likelihood. For example, what is the probability that a data recovery scheme will result in losing any business transactions? Four techniques are presented below:

   ☐ Odds — Estimate odds at or around the number 10, such as 6:1, 10:3, or 13:2.

   ☐ Log odds — Estimate odds based on a scale of 1 to 100.

   ☐ Log log odds — Estimate odds based on a scale of 1 to 1000.

   ☐ Probability — Use this more exacting quantitative technique for routine situations in which many measures are available; it should not be used for unique situations.

3. *Estimations of Magnitude* — When it is desirable to determine the magnitude of support for an alternative, any of the following techniques can be used:

☐ People's perceptions of magnitude — Rely upon subjective judgments, such as which alternatives are too costly, and which generate the needed support.

☐ Single-anchored worth — First establish a minimal acceptance criterion, like 24-hour data retrieval; then ask each person to estimate the value associated with any improvements. For example, how much are such improvements as twelve-hour, thirty-minute and three-second response times worth?

☐ Double-anchored worth — Do the same as above, except establish minimum and maximum limits for each criterion (such as cost, ease of use, or speed) and review each alternative to see how it fits the range.

☐ Indifference curves — Determine the point at which an individual is as likely to go one way as another. For example, if the cost of a computer terminal is $900, I know that I will support the on-line system alternative. If it costs $4,000 per unit, I will not support the alternative. However, at $3,300 per unit, I don't know how I'll decide — which means that at $3,300 per unit, some value other than terminal cost may sway my opinion.

4.2.3 Reaching a decision

Once data has been collected and properly aggregated, it is possible to begin the act of decision-making. Just as it was important not to jump from data collection to reaching a decision, it should be recognized that the final step of decision-making is distinct from data aggregation. The organization and quantification of results are helpful to the decision-makers, but do not, in themselves, represent group decisions.

Reaching a decision must involve the full range of criteria — social, political, and environmental — surrounding the issue. Thus, team members need to clarify which criteria are most important. For instance, perhaps management acceptance or clerical staff acceptance of the decision is most important. In any event, it is necessary to establish a single set of criteria before proceeding.

There are a number of ways in which the actual decision can be made. Schein has identified six of them, listed below in order of preference:

- unanimous consensus
- consensus
- majority rule
- minority rule (subgroup decision)
- authority rule
- lack of response (letting it die)[4]

For major decisions, it is recommended that the team not consider as viable anything less than majority rule. Even with a majority, it may be advisable in some instances to continue the decision-making process until a consensus can be reached.

The process of decision-making frequently can be time-consuming when major issues are at hand. The decision-making process is absolutely central to developing full-team participation, an environment characterized by openness between team members, and a sense of commitment to the team's goals, objectives, and recommendations.

4.3 Professional organization development strategies

The field of organization development (OD) is very broad, and offers strategies that can be used at various levels within an organization. In examining systems development teams, we are primarily concerned with the work style of the individual team members as it facilitates or impedes the team's ability to function effectively and achieve its goals. When a team is experiencing significant interpersonal and organizational problems, it is advisable to consider hiring an external OD consultant. In so doing, the organization is not acquiring an "expert" who will solve its problems and make major decisions. To the contrary, the task of the OD consultant is to assist the team in recognizing its problems and developing improved processes for dealing with these problems. The goal of the consultant is to make the team more effective, efficient, and self-sufficient in performing its work. Several of the more frequently used OD strategies for dealing with team problems are described below.

4.3.1 Process consultation

Schein, who has written the most definitive work on process consultation, has defined it as "a set of activities on the part of the consultant which help the client to perceive, understand and act upon process events which occur in the client's environment."* This definition implies that the consultant will have skill in establishing a "help" relationship with the client(s), knowing what kinds of processes need to be examined and intervening in a way that results in improved organizational processes. Schein has identified six process areas in which the process consultant can provide valuable diagnostic assistance.[5] Each is briefly described below:

Communications processes — Effective working relationships between team members and high team output are supported by effective interpersonal communications within the team. The process consultant analyzes the communications process in terms of the frequency, style (e.g., verbal or gestural), and level of communication.

Functional roles of group members — The different roles team members adopt (for instance, devil's advocate, critic, good Samaritan, facilitator, or savior) need to be supportive of both task achievement and of team maintenance activities, which sustain the team as a cohesive work group. The process consultant assists the team members to overcome such problems as excessive self-oriented behavior and internal power struggles. Specifically, the objectives of the process consultant are two: to help individual members determine a role that will enable them to satisfy personal needs while also working toward group goals, and to facilitate the team's analysis of its own performance in terms of both task achievement and team maintenance activities.

Group problem-solving and decision-making — This topic, covered quite fully in Section 4.2, represents an important focal point for the process consultant in helping the team to become more efficient and effective.

Group norms and group growth — The process consultant can assist the team by identifying the norms that the team has explicitly or implicitly developed. For example, the team may have advertently or inadvertently developed "non-confrontation" as an operating norm or rule for behavior. Also, the consultant may help the team to become more aware of the ways in which it has developed and matured, and the specific areas in which it needs further development.

---

*E.H. Schein, *Process Consultation: Its Role in Organization Development* (Reading, Mass.: Addison-Wesley, 1969), p. 9.

Leadership and authority — There are a wide variety of leadership styles. The function of the process consultant is to assist the team to understand and work with a variety of styles and to advise the leader to adjust his or her style to best fit a particular situation.

Intergroup processes — The relationship between the team and other groups may be characterized as either cooperative or competitive. The consequences of excessive competition between groups can be dysfunctional in terms of eventual costs/benefits to the total organization. The process consultant works actively with the team and management to avoid arranging reward structures that encourage excessive intergroup competitiveness.

In addition to providing diagnostic assistance, the process consultant utilizes a variety of interventions to assist the team in becoming a more effective work group. Schein has developed a broad categorization of these interventions, as follows:*

1. Agenda-setting interventions
   - questions that direct attention to interpersonal issues
   - process analysis periods
   - agenda review and testing procedures
   - meetings devoted to interpersonal process
   - conceptual inputs on interpersonal process topics

2. Feedback of observations or other data
   - feedback to groups during process analysis or regular work-time
   - feedback to individuals following meetings or data gathering

3. Coaching or counseling of individuals or groups

4. Structural suggestions
   - pertaining to group membership
   - pertaining to communication or interaction patterns
   - pertaining to allocation of work, assignment of responsibility, and lines of authority[6]

---

*This list is in the order of descending likelihood of use from Schein's perspective. That is, he would be most likely to intervene in setting the team's agenda and least likely to make structural suggestions.

Several of the basic tenets of process consultation are critical to successful use of teams in the development of information systems. First, the problems that teams experience are not only technical or applications-related. Rather, they are frequently linked to group dynamics and group processes.

Second, the team may have difficulty in identifying the existence of these group-related problems, since the team is usually preoccupied with systems development tasks and issues. Finally, the team members may not possess the necessary organizational expertise required to act upon these group process problems. It is increasingly common to assign a consultant or knowledgeable staff member to work with the team as a group process facilitator. Unlike other types of systems consultants, this individual does not provide the team with added technical or applications expertise. Rather, the individual's primary functions are to observe, analyze, and evaluate the ongoing group dynamics; and to assist the team in becoming a more effective work group.

In Part II, the reader will frequently assume the role of the facilitator. The objectives of that approach are to provide a framework for and practice in observing, analyzing, and evaluating team effectiveness, as well as to suggest activities that will improve overall team success.

4.3.2 Team-building strategies

Frequently, we discover after the fact that an existing team has not been working effectively; that is, it has not been producing the desired results within the needed time-frame. Historically, there has been a tendency to assume that technical competence is the primary factor in success or failure of the systems development effort. Thus, the solutions typically offered for getting the project back on schedule have stressed either augmenting the team with additional technically competent staff, or replacing staff with individuals deemed to be more technically competent.

An alternative approach would be to assess the extent to which organizational and group dynamics impede team progress. When these factors are found to be significant, simply adding new technically competent staff will not prove to be an effective strategy. Rather, it becomes crucial to develop a strategy to build the existing team into a more effective work group. Only then will it be able to achieve the desired task-related results within a reasonable time.

There are many possible approaches to team building, and those that are widely used generally focus on some aspect(s) of group behavior believed to be particularly critical. Referencing an unpublished manuscript by Beer, Huse describes four different models for team development: the goal-setting model, interpersonal model, role model, and managerial grid model.[7]

The *goal-setting model* for the team-building effort focuses on the establishment of group goals by reviewing current goals, establishing new goals, and developing strategies for implementing these goals. Joint participation in goal-setting is stressed, since that process has been demonstrated to raise team-member commitment and motivation to achieve the established goals. Goals may be established for both task achievement and team maintenance. The role of the OD consultant is very much that of a process consultant with a specific objective based upon the assumption that group goals are particularly influential in their impact upon group effort and behavior.

The *interpersonal model* is based upon the assumption that an interpersonally competent group is more effective than a group that lacks such competence. The objectives in team building are to increase mutual trust, supportiveness, confidence, and openness among team members. These objectives are not task-related. Rather, the focus is on creating a climate in which conflict is confronted, problems are solved effectively, and wise decisions are reached. The OD consultant generally collects data about the team's interpersonal interactions (either inside or outside the meeting), and then provides it as feedback to the team during the team-building meeting.

In the *role-model* effort, one or more team-building meetings is held to clarify team-member roles. The discussions may relate to task-specific roles, but also to more global issues such as leadership, power, or status. As a result, it is possible to identify which team members are experiencing role ambiguity because they do not clearly understand what is expected of them. Role clarification can result in an individual's experiencing greater personal satisfaction in performing team work. Most systems development team members have many roles; for example, a person may be a member of the development team and also be a supervisor in the budget office. If conflicts develop between these roles, the team member's effectiveness may be reduced. Identifying and resolving these role conflicts are objectives in this team-building model.

In the *Managerial Grid® model,* two components of individual behavior are assumed to be fundamentally important: concern for people, and concern for production. The grid or matrix in Fig. 4.2 displays five basic managerial styles.*

---

*The Managerial Grid figure is from *The New Managerial Grid,* by Robert R. Blake and Jane Srygley Mouton. Houston: Gulf Publishing Company, Copyright © 1978, p. 11. Reproduced by permission.

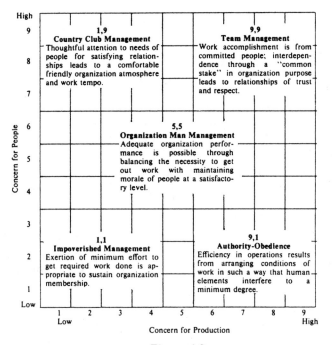

Figure 4.2

The use of the grid in OD work can occur at many levels in the organization; our interest is in its use in team-work development. The grid approach has six major objectives with regard to team work:

- institution of a problem-solving culture that has an "ideal" approach to problem-solving

- development of team-members' insights into their own behavior, using the grid as the frame of reference

- providing the team with objective standards of excellence and encouraging further development of the standards

- establishment of objectives both for individual team members and for the team as a whole

- improvement of team-work skills by assisting team members to acquire competence in making sound use of time, identifying and grasping problems, examining alternatives, opening up communications, and critiquing the soundness of proposed solutions

- learning to use the critique as a means of future improvement

Of these four very different role models for team development, the first three tend to be less packaged and rely more heavily upon the creative bent of the particular consultant, while the fourth approach is more packaged or prescriptive, in the sense of relying almost totally upon the assumptions inherent in the grid approach.

The decision to use an organizational consultant for team building is contingent upon the extent to which an organization possesses in-house OD expertise and the degree of problem severity. When there is no in-house expert or when the problem is acute, the systems development team could benefit from hiring a consultant who uses one or a combination of the team-building methods outlined above. Since consultants utilize a variety of approaches, the preceding brief descriptions should be used as a framework for clarifying and evaluating the kind of consulting service that is being proposed by any particular consultant.

4.4 Summary

This chapter has described practical suggestions to consider in attempting to maximize team performance. Many of the suggestions relate to the manner in which team meetings are organized and conducted. In addition to procedural issues such as building agenda, using chart pads, and so on, techniques that encourage active participation by all team members should be employed. Finally, there is a need for some formal training of systems developers in the area of interpersonal communications to help build skills required for effective performance with a team.

Many teams experience problems in the area of group decision-making. Remember that there are three stages in effective decision-making: data collection, data aggregation, and the final act of deciding. Each stage is important and should not be overlooked or treated lightly. While effective group decision-making requires time to achieve, it results in decisions that are broadly supported and consequently durable.

When a team is experiencing significant interpersonal and organizational problems, it is advisable to consider hiring an organization development consultant. Professional consultants use several OD strategies, such as process consultation, and a variety of team-building models, such as the goal-setting, interpersonal, role, and managerial grid models.

A team could expect to benefit from professional intervention using one or a combination of these OD strategies. As we have seen, maximizing team effectiveness requires that we first identify the underlying human and organizational issues that affect group work. By understanding in what areas teams are most likely to experience human and organizational problems, we are better able to construct or acquire an appropriate remedy. As the team gains experience in addressing and resolving team problems, it will become less reliant on external assistance. Further, the team will become more productive in achieving its technical and applications objectives, since it will have learned to deal more effectively with the fewer people and organizational problems that it encounters.

Chapter 4: References

1. P.C. Semprevivo, "A Critical Assessment of Team Approaches to Systems Development," *Proceedings of the Fifteenth Annual Computer Personnel Research Conference* (New York: Association for Computing Machinery, 1977), pp. 94−103.

2. J.K. Fordyce and R. Weil, *Managing with People* (Reading, Mass.: Addison-Wesley, 1971), pp. 157−67.

3. P.C. Semprevivo, *Systems Analysis* (Chicago: Science Research Assoc., 1976), pp. 323−26.

4. E.H. Schein, *Process Consultation: Its Role in Organization Development* (Reading, Mass.: Addison-Wesley, 1969), pp. 5, 46−58.

5. Ibid., pp. 3−8, 15−76.

6. Ibid., pp. 12, 102−22.

7. E.F. Huse, *Organization Development and Change* (St. Paul, Minn.: West Publishing, 1975), pp. 232−33.

Part II
A Practical Approach to Analyzing
and Evaluating Team Performance

". . . knowing afar off . . . the evils that are brewing, they
are easily cured. But when, for want to such knowledge,
they are allowed to grow so that everyone can recognize
them, there is no longer any remedy to be found."

— Niccolo Machiavelli
The Prince

A team is a dynamic entity. For the systems professional working
as a member of a development team, the many variables that can potentially affect team performance have a special significance. That is,
they directly influence one's professional achievement and success.
Thus, to trust in the belief that simply creating a team will somehow
result in improved systems development is tantamount to playing Rus-
sian Roulette with one's career. An alternative is to begin building a
base of knowledge about team interactions and to develop skill in
analyzing and evaluating team behavior. Using this approach, we can
diagnose potential problems before they reach the critical stages, and
can initiate appropriate action.

The goal of Part II of this text is to build a bridge between the
theory of teams and the application of that theory. The chapters in Part
II assume that the reader is either a member of a functioning team or
has reasonable access to a team with which he or she can work.
Specifically, Part II seeks to

- extend the reader's knowledge about teams through
  the introduction of additional research materials

- develop structured guidelines for data gathering and data evaluation that can be applied by the reader in a real-world situation

- relate team observation to prior discussions about problems experienced in developing large-scale information systems

- provide specific suggestions for dealing with common team problems

Factors that can affect team performance have been grouped into five major categories: organizational context, physical environment, team structure and member selection, social structure and interaction, and task environment and leadership. These categories provide the subject matter for the individual chapters comprising Part II.

Each chapter is organized in the following way: First, the major category is explained and some of the pertinent research findings are cited. Second, an analytical guide has been constructed to facilitate data gathering and analysis. The guide is constructed for use by the novice and provides a structure for obtaining important information about team members' interaction. While some benefit may be obtained by simply reading through the various questions and guidelines, the reader is encouraged to apply them to a real-world situation.

Following the analysis, an evaluative guide has been constructed to facilitate the reader's assimilation of the collected data. The guide is intended to relate team experiences both to the relevant research and to the Part I observations about why large-scale systems development efforts frequently encounter problems. Again, the reader will gain maximum benefit by working with an actual team in attempting to obtain answers to the evaluative questions posed in the guide.

Finally, each chapter concludes with practical suggestions and recommendations for improving team effectiveness.

Before proceeding, we must stress several important points regarding any attempt to analyze and evaluate team performance. First, because systems development teams are dynamic entities that function over long periods of time, we need to recognize that a single analysis and evaluation would be inappropriate. Thus, conducting an initial analysis and evaluation is only the first step toward what should become a program of ongoing concern for how well the team is performing.

The five categories of factors that can be used to evaluate team performance have been treated separately for purposes of clarity in presentation. As one gains knowledge about these factors and develops a sensitivity to the subtleties of their expression, they should serve as an aggregate or multidimensional framework within which to observe and evaluate team performance.

All factors will not be equally important for all teams or at all times in the life of the team. Provided here is the broad range of factors that influence team performance and thus require some degree of investigation. As a result of your use of the data collection and data evaluation guides, you should have a more precise understanding of which factors most significantly affect a given team's performance at a particular point in its life.

Working with systems development teams is a relatively new phenomenon. Previously, we briefly described some of the tools and techniques utilized by professional organization development practitioners. When severe small-group or team problems are detected, it is increasingly common for an organization to turn to the OD professional for assistance. While it is probably not always practical to stop a systems development project in mid-stream to engage in OD activities, sometimes it is the only rational alternative. Certainly, it is worth considering the possibility of requiring some OD intervention, and accounting for this possibility when a new project is in the planning stage.

Organizational Context | 5

One way to begin examining what a team is and how it functions is to view it as an organizational entity in its own right. In so doing, we properly regard the team as more than a mere collection of individuals, and view it as a primary social structure existing somewhere between the individual and the total business organization of which it is a part. This is a most important factor in understanding teams, because associated with it is an awareness that we must be concerned with team results at three levels:

- results that affect individual team members

- results that influence the group's operation and behavior

- results that affect the group's relationships with the rest of the organization[1]

Earlier in the text, we noted the general expectation that team approaches will result in greater productivity and, indeed, products of higher quality. We also expressed a concern that the design of new systems ought to better reflect the needs and expectations of those non-data processing personnel who will ultimately have responsibility for using the system. In the ideal sense, then, we would like to have synergistic teams producing very qualitative and utilitarian products. Were we able to find such a team, we could probably ascribe to it many specific positive results in its impact at all three organizational levels previously mentioned — individual, group, and total organization.

In fact, the ideal seldom happens. By focusing on the team as an organizational entity, we will gain a better understanding of specific problem areas and areas in which the team is most effective. Thus, for example, we will be able to differentiate between teams that simply work well as a group and those that are also effective in terms of the larger business organization. Overall success in the development and implementation of a new system will require at least some degree of team success in producing positive results at all three levels.

5.1 The team as an organizational structure

As previously noted, the evolution of database technology has resulted in more frequent attempts to develop large-scale information systems that cut across functional lines in an organization. While our focus in the past may have been on developing a payroll, accounts payable, or accounts receivable system, clearly our focus today would more likely be on producing a financial information system. This creates problems since the application (that is, the financial system) is cross-functional, while most business organizations are structured functionally such that each function has its own chain of command. The implication for developing a cross-functional system is very clear: There is no guarantee that all of the organizational units affected by the system will report to the same vice-president, let alone the same immediate supervisor. Indeed, the converse is more typically the case: The proposed system and the existing formal organization will not correspond.

Galbraith has described the team as a structural component that can be used to facilitate lateral communication across functional lines whenever a problem does not fit neatly into one functional area of an organization.[2] This important point of view helps to clarify conditions under which the team approach should be considered. It also helps us to appreciate that, in organizing a systems development team, we are introducing a new organizational entity; hence, care must be taken to ensure that

- the team is representative of the constituency it is designed to serve

- the team is properly linked to management of the total organization

- the team's objectives (its "turf," so to speak) are clearly identified and widely understood so as to minimize potential conflict

We will want to look closely at the organizational structure of the team to determine whether it is appropriate to the task and properly structured to fulfill its mission.

5.2 Team analysis: organizational context

Analyzing teams within their organizational context is a multistep process requiring rather specific data gathering. To facilitate this process, the following structured guidelines have been developed. The objective of our data collection is to gain specific knowledge regarding three categories:

- the project task and team members

- formal organizational relationships

- team actions or decisions and their impact on the individual, group, and total organization

Consequently, the data collection guide is structured as a three-step process, each step corresponding to one of these categories.

5.2.1 Data collection

Step 1: Select a systems development team of which you are a member or to which you have reasonable access. Do the following:

☐ Describe the task or project on which the team is working. Be specific with regard to the work phase, that is, analysis, design, and so on.

☐ List the functional areas (payroll or accounts payable, for example) that will be affected by the new system.

☐ Identify each of the team members and provide the information specified below:

Name/Title	Organizational Unit	Full or Part-time Member	Reason for Selection*	Percentage of Team Meetings Not Attended

*A single word or phrase, such as "special knowledge," "decision-maker," or "previous experience," will suffice.

Step 2: Complete an organizational chart that shows chain-of-command relationships between team members. Also show how people rank in the overall hierarchy relative to one another. Place the initials of each member in the appropriate box and draw connecting lines as required. For example,

Step 3: Construct a list of specific decisions or actions taken by the team recently.

☐ Ask each team member to evaluate each decision/action in terms of his own personal feelings. Categories of response should include: (1) very satisfied, (2) satisfied, (3) neutral, (4) dissatisfied, (5) very dissatisfied, and (6) did not participate in the decision/action; you may also allow for some free-form personal expression. Tabulate the results in a separate chart for each team member, as shown below:

Evaluator's initials:		
Team Action/ Decision	Rating	Team Member's Personal Feelings (Free-form)

☐ Ask each team member how he feels most other team members would respond if asked to evaluate the same decisions/actions. Use the response categories given above. Tabulate the results for each member in the format illustrated below:

Evaluator's initials:		
Team Action/ Decision	Rating	Assessment of Other Team Members' Feelings

☐ Ask each team member how he feels most non-team users and management would evaluate these decisions/actions. Use the following response categories: (1) strongly agree with the team decision, (2) agree, (3) wouldn't care, (4) disagree, (5) strongly disagree, and (6) wouldn't know about the decision/action. Tabulate the results for each member in the format illustrated below:

		Evaluator's initials:
Team Action/ Decision	Rating	Assessment of Management's and Users' Feelings

At this point, you should have acquired a useful preliminary base of data about the team. Certainly, the data will be helpful in our evaluation of how effectively the team is performing from the perspective of the organizational context. Also, because teams are dynamic and highly interactive entities, we will find this data to have value in later examinations of other factors that can have an impact on team performance. In effect, it represents the beginning of a database about a team's performance, which will grow as we work through the remainder of this text.

5.3 Evaluation of the analysis: organizational context

Working with the data that has been collected thus far, we can pose some evaluative questions regarding the organizational context of the team. The answers you provide to these questions will form a basis for assessing the relative strengths and weaknesses inherent in the team's organization, and thus its potential for success or failure.

Throughout this evaluative process, it is important to keep in perspective those broader issues presented in Part I, regarding the reasons that systems development efforts frequently fail. Also, keep in mind the theory of teams presented at the beginning of this chapter. To the extent possible, reference will be made to those issues and ideas for each subset of evaluative questions.

5.3.1 Evaluative questions about team constituency

We would expect a study of the team approach to deal with the relative lack of management and user involvement during the systems development process. Similarly, we would expect the membership of the team to reflect the areas to be affected by the new system as well as to represent top management. Answers to the questions below will provide insight into how effective the organization of your team has been in addressing these issues.

☐ Of the areas that will be affected by the system, which do/do not have formal representation on the team?

Areas Affected	Number of Team Members	Full- or Part-time

☐ If there are imbalances, how important do you judge them to be?

☐ Are there other formal or informal links to groups not represented or under-represented? Suggest a few.

☐ Are people with the necessary information and decision-making authority on the team?

☐ If you could start over again or recommend sweeping change, what team makeup would you recommend?

5.3.2 Evaluative questions about team-member relationships

The questions raised in this section are more subtle than ones posed in the preceding sections, because these pertain to the broader issue of user/management participation. In effect, we will attempt to determine if there are organizational factors and prior work relationships that could impact equality of participation by the team members, or the balance of influence that particular points of view can be expected to have.

Providing answers to these questions should make you better able to assess any organizational bias inherent in the team's structure. This should be helpful in determining those external groups with which the team will be most and/or least effective.

☐ Do direct supervisory relationships exist between members? Do they affect who participates, or result in the formation of cliques?

☐ Do team members represent different levels in the organizational hierarchy? Does this affect the extent of participation and/or the degree of influence of the individual team members?

☐ Are team members drawn from the same organizational unit outside of the team? Does this determine who participates, or does it cause the formation of cliques?

☐ Are there pre-existing authority structures that could predispose the team toward a central authority structure?

☐ If you could start over again or recommend sweeping change, how would you construct the team differently in terms of member relationships?

5.3.3 Evaluative questions about team decisions and actions

We have already noted that systems development occurs within very real time constraints. Dissatisfaction and dissent within the team can create conflicts and significant delays in achieving the primary goal of a new system. On the positive side, uniform commitment and a sense of the importance with which others view the project would be advantageous for getting the job done in a timely fashion. Because of this benefit, it becomes important to evaluate individual, group, and organizational perceptions about the work of the team.

A word of caution is advisable at this point: These perceptions may vary depending upon the particular issue, decision, or action being discussed. Take care not to obscure these points of difference in your final assessments, since they represent potential impediments to team effectiveness.

☐ What is the extent of personal dissatisfaction among team members regarding the team's actions and decisions?

☐ When you compare personal feelings to perceptions about how others feel, are there discrepancies?

☐ When you compare personal and team feelings to those views perceived to be held by management and other users, are there discrepancies?

☐ Are external users and management aware of and concerned with the team's actions and decisions?

☐ How do the feelings of individual team members relate to what you discovered in Steps 1 and 2 of this evaluation? (For example, do imbalances in representation correlate with positive or negative feelings? Are people in higher-level positions generally more positive or less positive than others?)

☐ Which team actions and decisions do you feel ought to be re-evaluated, based upon your findings?

5.4 Practical suggestions

The purpose of this and similar sections throughout Part II is to review briefly the results of the analysis and evaluation, and to illustrate how they might be used to improve team effectiveness. If serious problems are discovered within the team, the primary use of this data might be to support a proposal to bring in a professional organizational specialist to work with the group, as discussed in Chapter 4.

Frequently, your analysis and evaluation can be a useful instrument in assisting the team to become more aware of its problems. If so, the team may be willing to spend at least some time in discussing and attempting to resolve these problems.

In doing this, it would be best to set aside some time specifically to discuss the analysis and evaluation findings. The amount of time should be limited since the team must continue to deal with its day-to-day agenda of development activities. In effect, you will be using your findings to stimulate discussion about issues such as

● How well are we doing as a team?

● Do we have problems and, if so, what are they and how important are they?

● What can we do to deal with those problems more effectively?

Keep in mind that others on the team may have their own interpretation of the data you present and of its significance. Also, it is important that you provide them with this information in the form of feedback, not a series of conclusions.

Some specific factors and alternatives to consider relate to the three major aspects of the evaluation. For example, if it becomes apparent that the team is not representative, you may want the team to consider what formal or informal adjustments could be made to the membership. Membership frequently can be extended rather quickly by securing part-time or liaison relationships with key people.

The aspects of team-member relationships evaluated in this chapter are preliminary to understanding a very complex issue involving organizational structure: communications and leadership. For example, if both the Director of Personnel/Payroll and the Payroll Supervisor who reports to the director are members of the same team, this may or may not represent a problem. It is, however, a clue that we must be especially sensitive to the possibility that the relationship will result in a less open participation by the Payroll Supervisor, that it will foster the development of a subgroup coalition, or that it will result in a tendency toward centralized leadership. In Chapters 8 and 9, we will look at communications and leadership aspects of team performance, and, thus, develop this theme more fully.

In analyzing how people feel or how they think others feel about team decisions and actions, we may discover both consistencies and inconsistencies that can be objectively shared with the team. For example, there may be times when a team member feels negatively about a particular action, but perceives that others are very positive about it. In reality, an evaluation may reveal that all of the team members share in this same misconception, and that they only agreed to the action because they thought it was supported by everyone else. At other times, individual team members may erroneously believe that their opinions about an action represent the majority point of view.

The relationship between the team and other groups within the organization is critical in several respects. First, consistency between group actions and the expectations of management and other user groups is important to the long-term success of the systems development effort. Second, the perceptions of those external groups influence the team's perception of itself. Finally, a lack of interest in the group's actions by management may forebode future difficulties in obtaining resource and other commitments to make the project a success. If there are discrepancies between team perceptions and those ascribed to others, it may be advisable for the team to develop a strategy for improving its organizational links to these groups. Suffice it to say that the team will almost certainly gain added insight about itself and the feelings of its members by discussing the results of your organizational analysis and evaluation.

Chapter 5: References

1. E.F. Huse, *Organization Development and Change* (St. Paul, Minn.: West Publishing, 1975), pp. 230–32.

2. J.R. Galbraith, *Organization Design* (Reading, Mass.: Addison-Wesley, 1977), p. 53.

Physical Environment | 6

The physical environment is a powerful factor in determining whether and how people work together. The traditional lack of consideration given this factor by management is evidenced by the fact that many systems development teams are not even allocated permanent space in which to meet and work. While this may not be significant for programming teams whose members routinely share a common office space, it is extremely significant for development teams made up of managers, users, and systems personnel who may have permanent office space distant from one another.

As we begin to analyze the physical environment in which the team operates, remember that there probably are limitations on one's ability to recommend broad changes to that environment to make it optimal for the team. Most organizations simply resist making these sorts of changes. Asking departments to give up or adjust their use of space is a territorial infringement. Consequently, a team's concern should be focused upon understanding and maximizing its use of the existing physical environment.

In analyzing and evaluating a team's physical environment, we can examine how the physical process of human interaction can influence the ways in which a team organizes itself; who will emerge as the team leader; and whether intrateam and interteam communications will prove effective. Thus, our discussion of the physical environment should further build upon the prior results of our study of the organizational context of teams. Furthermore, the data collected in this chapter will prove helpful in providing a basis for evaluating team performance in future chapters.

For systems development teams, we will concern ourselves with three primary dimensions of the physical environment issue, as listed on the following page.

- spatial-physical barriers
- communications channel networks
- environmental cues

Each of these factors is discussed below, followed by sections on analysis and evaluation of the physical environment and practical suggestions for improving the physical environment of teams.

6.1 Spatial-physical barriers

Any number of rather obvious physical and spatial barriers can be observed within an organization. Melcher has suggested that these barriers be grouped into the following three major categories:

- separation by distance
- separation by semi-fixed features, such as tables, chairs, and so on
- separation by fixed features, such as walls[1]

He further points out that these barriers impede people's interaction with one another, thus altering communication patterns within an organization. At times, the impact of these barriers upon communications is an involuntary one, resulting primarily from the original design of the physical facility and the placement of individuals within that design. However, at other times, individuals purposefully use these existing barriers or even add to them, possibly resulting in communication breakdowns between some team members or in the formation of cliques. Such intentional use of spatial-physical barriers may serve to increase in-group cohesion, as well as to intensify barriers between the team and external groups.

While the process of identifying and describing the kinds of spatial-physical barriers that may exist in the physical environment of a team is rather straightforward, the consequences of reducing or increasing these barriers is far more complex. While reducing the barriers between people or groups will generally result in greater interaction between those affected by the change, the consequences may be desirable or not depending upon pre-existing conditions. For example, if conflict existed between these individuals or groups prior to the barrier reduction, we can expect that conflict will increase once the barriers are removed. Of course, if there previously was cooperation between the individuals or groups, then we might reasonably expect the degree of cooperation to increase as a result of the barrier reduction. Melcher's diagram summarizing the relationship between pre-existing conditions, specific action to increase or remove barriers, and the possible consequences of that action is provided below (see Fig. 6.1).*

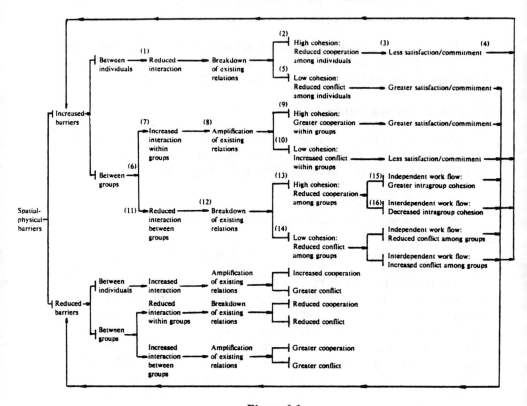

Figure 6.1

In order to address the practical aspects of analyzing and evaluating the impact of the physical environment on teams, it will be necessary to exercise caution in recommending specific environmental changes unless we can determine that the action will result in positive consequences. Hence, we will need to have some understanding of the pre-existing conditions between people and groups. Avoid the rather naive assumption that reducing the spatial-physical barriers between team members will result in greater cooperation between them.

*Arlyn J. Melcher, *Structure and Process of Organizations: A Systems Approach,* © 1976, p. 139. Reprinted by permission of Prentice-Hall, Inc., Englewood Cliffs, N.J.

6.2 Communications channel networks

A second dimension to the physical environment issue has been presented by Shaw and refers to the number and arrangement of communications channels in the organization.[2] The distribution of these channels throughout an organization determines how communications will occur. In this sense, an individual's physical environment is defined by the boundaries of his ability to communicate effectively and easily with others. With regard to systems development teams, we will want to identify the communications channels that function within the team, and between the team and important external individuals and groups, such as top management.

There are various kinds of communications networks that might exist for a team. It is helpful to think of these possible alternatives as representing a continuum. At one end of the continuum, we could have a highly centralized communications structure in which most or all of the communicating is to or through a single member of the team. In such an arrangement, this central figure will likely emerge as the team leader.

At the other end of our continuum, we would find a highly decentralized communications network, in which each member of the team would tend to communicate directly with all other members of the team. In Chapter 5, we discussed two factors that could result in a more highly centralized communications structure: pre-established authority relationships between members of the team (that is, one member is the direct supervisor of another), and prior working relationships between two or more members of the team. A third factor, the physical environment, can also have an impact. For example, if it is physically easier for all members of a team to communicate through one individual, then a centralized communications network will evolve, and that individual will most likely emerge as the team leader.

There is a common misconception that good project management and centralized communications networks are synonymous. To some extent, the previously referenced chief programmer team concept[3] and the long-standing systems development practice of appointing a strong project leader to head a development team make this same mistake. After reviewing the results of numerous studies of small-group behavior, Shaw developed a series of hypotheses, three of which are particularly pertinent to a study of systems development teams:

- group members have higher morale in decentralized than in centralized communications networks

- a decentralized communications network is more efficient for the group in solving complex problems and less efficient in solving simple problems

- a centralized communications network is more vulnerable to saturation or overloading and, hence, breaking down than is a decentralized network[4]

With regard to Shaw's third hypothesis, note that a team developing a large-scale system must make literally thousands of specific decisions about the new system. While the team leader may be expected to facilitate the team's work by effectively scheduling people and activities, this does not mean that the team leader should be solely responsible for decision-making and intrateam communication. To the contrary, the possibility for overloading or saturating the project leader in a centralized network arrangement would be very high indeed — to the detriment of the project.

6.3 Environmental cues

In analyzing the physical environment, we are, in part, observing something that simply reflects the predominant beliefs and attitudes of the individual team members. For example, where people sit at a meeting room table, whom they sit next to, and the frequency of verbal exchange between them may be important indicators of where cooperation and/or conflict reside within the team.

Naturally, it is possible to attach too much significance to these factors — but that has not traditionally been the problem. To the contrary, a virtual disregard of the significance of these important cues has been the standard until recently.

By remaining sensitive to these cues in the physical environment, we can obtain an early warning that a team is having problems in working as a cohesive group.

6.4 Team analysis: physical environment

In analyzing the physical environment of a team, we are partly studying the way in which the physical environment affects communications processes, which in turn can have wide-ranging effects upon the structure and effectiveness of the team.

In this section, you will perform a series of data collection and analysis activities on the team under investigation. A set of guidelines has been constructed to assist you in this task. These guidelines center on four rather specific objectives: First, you will document the physical environment per se. Second, you will observe how people interact in that environment. Next, you will assess how the environment may have influenced the way in which the team is structured. Last, you will want to assess how other team members feel about the physical environment. Some of the activities, such as noting where people sit during a meeting, may require several observations before patterns of behavior become evident.

6.4.1 Data collection

Step 1: Develop one or a series of diagrams that illustrate the extent to which the barriers of distance, semi-fixed features, and fixed features exist in the team's physical environment.

☐ For contiguous office areas, provide team-member office layouts indicating locations of barriers and people.

☐ For non-contiguous space, portray the extent to which barriers exist between team members. Below is an attempt to show the relative distance between people in a mythical office.

KEY

1″ = 150′

☐ Note the relative proximity of each team member to the usual formal meeting and group-work rooms. Make a note if there is no official place designated for this purpose or if a particular team member's office has been so designated.

Member	Distance

Step 2: Attend a number of formal meetings of the group. Note where people sit at the meeting table as indicated below.

☐ Examine if there is a pattern as to who sits at the head of the table, and which people regularly sit next to, adjacent to, or across from one another.

☐ Record relative frequency of verbal exchange between persons. One easy way of doing this is to diagram the seating plan. Draw lines between people indicating direct communication, and darken the lines between two people as they increase their frequency of verbal exchange.

☐ Determine the extent to which people communicate with one another outside of the formal meeting room. Ask each member to rate the other team members on the frequency with which they communicate face to face, on the telephone, or in writing. For example, using a rating of 1 (highest) to 4 (lowest), present your results as illustrated below:

TEAM MEMBER	1	2	3	4	5
1	0				
2		0			
3			0		
4				0	
5					0

Step 3: Ask questions about team structure.

☐ Instruct each team member to rank all members (self-inclusive) on the basis of each person's influence on team decisions. Determine composite scores for each member.

☐ Ask each team member to rank all members (self-inclusive) on the basis of each one's influence on groups external to the team. Determine composite scores for each member.

☐ Ask each team member to rank all members (self-inclusive) on the basis of special skills and knowledge essential to getting the job done. Determine composite scores for each member.

☐ Ask each member to name the appointed leader, and then the true leader of the team. Tabulate total votes for each member.

☐ Ask members with whom they work most frequently, and with whom they most like and/or dislike working. Tabulate data for each member.

☐ Ask each team member to rate the effectiveness of the leadership within the group, using a scale of one to five (one being most effective, and five being least). What is the average leadership-effectiveness rating?

Step 4: Ask questions about opinions on the physical environment.

☐ Were any office or other changes executed as a direct result of the team's formation?

☐ Did team members have a voice in selecting the physical environment in which they must function?

☐ Do the team members feel that the physical environment is conducive to the team's work? If not, ask each team member to describe the problems, using the categories of distance barriers, semi-fixed barriers, fixed barriers, and communications problems.

☐ Are there changes that would improve the physical environment?

6.5 Evaluation of the analysis: physical environment

In Part I of this text, concern was expressed regarding who makes decisions about a new system, and regarding effective project management, the informal organization, and the setting of realistic expectations for a systems development effort.

Using the data collected in the previous analysis, we can answer a series of evaluative questions, presented below, which pertain to the team's physical environment. These data will tell us how effective management has been in creating a physical environment that is supportive of the team's work. We should also begin to see how the physical environment might result in an informal communications network, which may not be apparent to people outside of the team.

6.5.1 Evaluative questions about the physical layout

☐ What barriers of distance, semi-fixed features, and fixed features are most apparent?

☐ Which of these would you judge to be most significant as (1) unintended barriers to effective communications? (2) self-imposed protective barriers?

☐ What changes do you believe could be made to remove the barriers? Do you feel the impact would be positive or negative?

☐ Are there any factors about the group meeting/work area that might predispose the team toward a centralized communications structure?

6.5.2 Evaluative questions about team interaction

As we look more specifically at how team members interact with one another, a number of evaluative questions can be asked to help clarify the relationship between the physical environment and how the team functions both formally and informally. Furthermore, the results of this evaluation should permit us to begin to identify whether the goal of full systems/user/management participation is being realized; areas of conflict within the group; and the extent to which centralized versus decentralized communications patterns have developed.

Answer the following evaluative questions:

☐ Are there similarities between a lack of physical barriers and seating arrangements in a formal meeting? Detail them.

☐ Are there correlations between where people sit in relation to one another and how frequently they engage in discussion at a meeting? Describe them.

☐ Are there any relationships between lack of physical barriers and how frequently and in what way people communicate with one another? Detail them.

☐ Are there regular patterns to where people sit at the table in formal meetings? Does one particular team member always sit at the head of the table?

6.5.3 Evaluative questions about team structure

In subsequent chapters, we shall discuss some of the criteria used to select team members and a team leader who will be effective both within the team and in its relationships to important external individuals and groups. At that time, we will more clearly see how influence (both internal and external), special skills and knowledge, specific leadership style, and strong interpersonal skills can determine a team member's effectiveness and leadership potential. Before proceeding to those issues, we first should understand that the physical environment can affect how people and their performance are perceived. A study of how people interact in a group can be helpful in revealing those perceptions.

Ask the following questions, which have been constructed to help you better determine what, if any, significant relationships exist for the team under investigation.

☐ How do individual and team assessments of influence within the team relate to

○ existence of physical barriers
○ seating arrangement at formal meetings
○ frequency and type of communication
○ frequency of verbal exchange during meetings

☐ How do individual and team assessments of influence outside the team relate to

○ existence of physical barriers
○ seating arrangement at formal meetings
○ frequency and type of communication
○ frequency of verbal exchange during meetings

☐ How do individual and team assessments of skills and knowledge relate to

○ existence of physical barriers
○ seating arrangement at formal meetings
○ frequency and type of communication
○ frequency of verbal exchange during meetings

☐ Is there general agreement on who the formal and true leaders are?

☐ For both the formal and true leaders, determine the following:

○ Are there physical barriers between them and others?
○ Where does each normally sit in a meeting?
○ What is the frequency and type of communication between them?
○ With whom does each interact most at meetings?

☐ How do individual preferences for working partners relate to

○ existence of physical barriers
○ seating arrangement at formal meetings
○ frequency and type of communication
○ frequency of verbal exchange during meetings

☐ Based on the data that you have collected, how would you judge the formal and true leaders in terms of

○ accessibility (lack of physical barriers)
○ communication
○ influence (internal and external)
○ knowledge
○ recognition (leadership acknowledgment within the team)
○ team-member support (e.g., being viewed as an effective leader)

6.5.4 Evaluative questions on feelings about the physical environment

Sound management of a systems development project seems to require that the project team be provided with a physical environment that is supportive of its task, and the fullest cooperation and participation of its membership. In evaluating the effectiveness of your team, think broadly about whether the physical environment is supportive, and how it can be made more supportive of the team's efforts. The following set of evaluative questions should assist you toward achieving this end:

☐ In your opinion, is the physical environment conducive to performance of the team's work?

☐ In your opinion, is maximal use being made of the existing physical environment?

☐ If the group is a cohesive one, what changes might be made to facilitate working together as a team?

☐ If the group is not cohesive, what changes might be made to minimize existing conflict?

☐ How might team members improve the physical environment in which they must work?

6.6 Practical suggestions

The physical layout of the work space can be a powerful factor in influencing overall team effectiveness and in shaping the manner in which members of the team interact. To some degree, one can expect that the existence or lack of barriers in the work environment will carry over to the extent and manner of communication in formal meetings or in day-to-day communications patterns. For example, it is not uncommon for people who work closely with one another also to sit near one another in meetings. While this appears, in and of itself, to be quite innocuous, extensions of this carry-over may not be. If the physical environment encourages it, cliques may form within the team. Existence of a clique signifies that all members of the team are not communicating equally well with one another.

By sharing your observations with the team, it may become apparent that many of the little idiosyncracies of the physical environment are, in fact, accurate reflections of

- who is communicating effectively with whom
- where potential or actual conflict resides within the group
- who has authority and influence within the group
- what preferences exist for working with others
- who is the true team leader
- how people feel about themselves as a result of where they work

If the physical environment appears to exert a negative influence upon the extent and quality of team-member interaction, it will become necessary either to alter the physical environment or to develop methodologies and facilities that help to compensate. For example, installing intercoms or scheduling more frequent group-work sessions may result in more evenly distributed communications.

Left unattended, the physical environment can result in a team structure that places potentially valuable team members on the periphery. Team members' perceptions about who has knowledge, skill, and influence may be more reflective of environmental circumstances than of fact. If this problem is evident, it may be necessary to develop a contravening strategy that brings to everyone's attention the potentially unique and valuable contributions of peripheral members. For example, manipulating the physical environment or making assignments that require increased interaction with others may be necessary to effect such a transition.

Negative feelings by team members about their working environment may interfere with their effectiveness. At times, this can involve highly personal feelings about security, self-worth, and a sense of achievement. If the business organization places the team in a work environment that is drab and unappealing, team members may interpret this as indicative of how management feels about them as individuals and about the relative significance of the project. Many things can be done to make the physical environment more pleasant and conducive to work, at very little cost. Fresh paint, some extra shelving, and a few prints on the wall could provide an incentive to the team members, themselves, to further improve upon the existing environment.

Chapter 6: References

1. A.J. Melcher, *Structure and Process of Organizations: A Systems Approach* (Englewood Cliffs, N.J.: Prentice-Hall, 1976), pp. 6, 117—44.

2. M.E. Shaw, *Group Dynamics* (New York: McGraw-Hill, 1976), pp. 5, 113—53.

3. F.T. Baker and H.D. Mills, "Chief Programmer Teams," *Datamation*, Vol. 19, No. 12 (December 1973), pp. 58—61. [Reprinted in E.N. Yourdon, ed., *Classics in Software Engineering* (New York: YOURDON Press, 1979), pp. 195—204.]

4. M.E. Shaw, op. cit., pp. 152—53.

Team Structure and Member Selection | 7

One of the ways in which we can gain a deeper understanding of systems development teams is to examine them as relatively autonomous work groups. Actually, such a point of view would be very consistent with the prevailing practice of utilizing a project approach to systems development. What has been lacking in many of our practical attempts at implementing a project strategy is a clear understanding of what it takes for a work group to become a reasonably autonomous team, as opposed to simply an ad hoc committee. Hackman has identified these essential characteristics of an autonomous work group:

- assignment of a whole task that the group views as significant and with which it can identify

- existence of the necessary skills and abilities required to perform the work

- decision-making autonomy with regard to work methods, job scheduling, and even perhaps selection of new or replacement team members

- compensation on the basis of group, versus individual, performance[1]

If we were to evaluate most project teams on the above criteria, we would probably conclude that they lacked many of the characteristics of an autonomous group.

In this chapter and in the subsequent two chapters, we will examine several dimensions of teams that directly or indirectly support the theory that functioning as an autonomous work group is prerequisite to becoming an effective team.

7.1 Team structure

Two structural issues — team size and heterogeneity — were not dealt with in Hackman's list, because they are not unique to autonomous work groups. They are, nonetheless, very important to effective team performance, and set limits and direction for the actual selection of team members.

The size of a work group is a most significant aspect of team structure and has impact both on group performance and on individual member satisfaction in problem-solving situations. In a study of the relationship between group size and individual member satisfaction, Harrison found that as the size of a group increased, so did individual member dissatisfaction.[2] Thus, individuals were most satisfied with membership in a small group (5 to 7 persons), and least satisfied in a large group (12 to 15 persons). If we apply this concept to systems development teams, it would appear that the alleged benefits of broader participation achievable with large groups would be more than offset by reduced levels of individual participation, coordination problems, and difficulties in achieving consensus.

While this is a most important point, it does revert us to the dilemma posed in Chapter 2: How does one increase staffing to reflect the work requirements of a large-scale project while also maintaining the conceptual cohesiveness of a small group of highly skilled and highly motivated individuals?[3] If we again turn to the research literature on this topic, we can obtain some guidelines on the matter. Marquis suggests that a small team of full-time personnel supplemented by many part-time participants will lead to superior performance.[4] Placed within the context of systems development teams, these results suggest a strategy of first establishing a highly motivated and highly skilled team of five or so people. This core team would then identify those external experts who would be needed to work on specific aspects of the development. Naturally, the core team would need the part-time commitment from the other participants early in the project.

We have previously discussed heterogeneity in terms of development teams made up of representatives from various organizational units. There are obviously many other characteristics, such as age and sex, that make a team either homogeneous or heterogeneous. Rather than provide an extensive analysis, characteristic by characteristic, suffice it to say that there appears to be support for the notion that a variety of options, backgrounds, and technical specialities will result in better solutions to a problem. Since systems development efforts frequently involve a diversity of technologies and must ultimately serve a broad constituency, they seem to benefit from a heterogeneous membership.

7.2 Team-member selection

The selection of team members is probably the single most influential event in the life of the team, and represents an opportunity to bring together the best possible group of people to do the job. It is also the opportunity that, in systems development, we have traditionally allowed to slip away. Many times, for example, the people we would like to have work on a team are "too busy," and we settle for less. At other times, we select too narrowly on the basis of formal positions.

To be done properly, the selection of team members should be approached from several directions simultaneously. In this chapter, we intend to discuss three approaches that together provide a sufficiently broad base of information from which to make good selections:

- organizational considerations
- team considerations
- individual considerations

As Galbraith has pointed out, team members must have the authority to commit their departments.[5] Also, they should have influence within the organization and possess project-related knowledge and skills. These three organizational realities must be heavily weighed in the evaluation process, but they are not the only criteria.

In discussing group effectiveness, Harrison points to the importance of interpersonal consensus within the group as playing a major role in determining cohesiveness and, hence, overall effectiveness.[6] This suggests that strong interpersonal skills, a common interest in the team objectives, and agreement that team goals are significant join to form a second subset of selection criteria.

Looking even further into the matter, we have sound reason to believe that certain personal characteristics and work styles can affect the team in different ways. Shaw has set forth a number of hypotheses about how different personal traits may affect groups.[7] For example, he states that more intelligent members are usually more active in the group and less conforming than less intelligent members; the more dependable the member, the more probable that he or she will emerge as a leader and help the group achieve its goal; the unconventional (unpredictable) member inhibits group functioning; the anxious group member inhibits group functioning, while the well-adjusted group member contributes to effective group functioning. Certainly, we do not typically perform batteries of personality tests prior to team selection, nor is that proposed. Rather, we simply point out that research does support the conventional notion that team members who are intelligent, dependable, socially sensitive, and well-adjusted will facilitate the team's attainment of its objectives.

7.3 Team analysis: team structure and member selection

In our prior analyses, the data collection activities were primarily structured for you to obtain new or first-time data. While that practice will continue to some extent, many of the activities will require that you re-analyze previously collected data from a different perspective. If, at times, you feel that additional discussions with specific individuals would provide a better base of data to work with, you should take the initiative in that direction.

The structure that has been provided to assist in this aspect of the analysis has several objectives. First, there is a need for you to collect some additional data about the team's composition. Steps 1 through 4 of the analysis focus on the organizational, team, and individual factors that ought to influence the selection of team members. Following this, you will be asked to construct a composite profile for the team with which you have been working. Finally, you will be asked to make an analysis of the team as an autonomous work group.

7.3.1 Data collection

Step 1: Collect the following information about team composition:

☐ Determine the full-time/part-time size of the team.

☐ Describe the composition of the team in terms of

    ○ sex
    ○ ethnicity
    ○ age group (that is, less than 25, 26-35, and so on)
    ○ organizational unit

☐ Examine each of the organizational units from which team members were selected, and tabulate their composition in terms of

    ○ sex
    ○ ethnicity
    ○ age groups (as before)

Step 2: Do the following based upon information previously obtained and any additional data you might wish to collect:

- ☐ Make your own assessment (scale from 1 = low to 5 = high) of each team member regarding
  - ○ authority to commit department
  - ○ influence in the total organization based upon knowledge and information
  - ○ possession of special, project-related skills and knowledge

- ☐ Summarize these results in chart form, indicating member and team totals.

Member Name	Authority	Influence	Project Knowledge	Member Total
Team Total				

Step 3: Do the following based upon observation, information previously collected, and/or additional data you might wish to collect:

- ☐ Make your own assessment (scale from 1 = low to 5 = high) of each team member regarding
  - ○ interpersonal skill level
  - ○ extent to which team objectives are shared by that individual
  - ○ extent to which individual feels team goals are important

- ☐ Summarize these results in chart form, indicating member and team totals.

Member Name	Interpersonal	Shared Objectives	Goal Importance	Member Total
Team Total				

Step 4: Do the following based upon observation, information previously collected, and/or additional data you might wish to collect:

☐ Make your own assessment (scale from 1 = low to 5 = high) of each team member regarding

    ○ general intelligence
    ○ dependability
    ○ social sensitivity
    ○ degree to which the individual is well-adjusted

☐ Summarize these results in chart form indicating member and team totals.

Member Name	Intelligence	Dependability	Sensitivity	Well-Adjusted	Member Total
Team Total					

Step 5: Using the member totals from the three previous steps, construct a summary chart as indicated below:

Member Name	Organizational Step 2	Team Step 3	Personal Step 4	Member Total
Team Total				

Step 6: Make your own assessment (scale from 1 = low to 5 = high) of the extent to which the team reflects each of the criteria for an autonomous work group.

☐ The systems development team

   ○ has been assigned a whole task _____ (a.1)
   ○ views its task as significant _____ (a.2)
   ○ can identify with its task _____ (a.3)

☐ The systems development team possesses the necessary skills and abilities needed to perform the work. _____ (b)

☐ The systems development team possesses decision-making autonomy with regard to

   ○ work methods used _____ (c.1)
   ○ job scheduling _____ (c.2)
   ○ selection of new and replacement team members _____ (c.3)

☐ The systems development team is rewarded on the basis of group versus individual performance. _____ (d)

☐ Enter the total scores for (a) through (d) in the table below and perform the indicated arithmetic:

Item	Raw Score	Multiple Factor	Total Scores
a		× 1	
b		× 3	
c		× 1	
d		× 3	
Total			

7.4 Evaluation of the analysis: team structure and member selection

Using the available data, we now can begin to pose some important evaluative questions regarding team structure and the selection of team members. The answers that you provide to these questions will form a basis for further assessing the strengths and weaknesses of the team.

Also, with this particular evaluation, we will begin to strike at some of the less formal and consequently less visible aspects of team performance. Whenever possible, we will attempt to draw parallels to the Part I discussions of problems involved in large-scale systems development efforts.

7.4.1 Evaluative questions about team composition

Earlier, we expressed concerns about who should participate in systems development, how many people should comprise a team, and what the quality of individual participation should be. We mentioned that one of the reasons for resistance to participation might well be previous, disappointing experiences. Therefore, every effort should be made to assure that the team experience is personally and professionally satisfying for the participants.

In our brief review of relevant literature on team structure, it became evident that team size, use of both full-time and part-time participants, and heterogeneity are significant factors that directly relate to the concerns expressed above.

By answering the following questions, you should gain some insight into how your team ranks on these important structural components.

- [ ] Does the size of the team fall within the guidelines mentioned?

- [ ] Has the team considered using an approach that maintains a small, full-time core team, supplemented by a broader base of part-time participants?

- [ ] Is the composition of the group representative of the organization in terms of age, sex, and ethnicity?

- [ ] What specific changes in team composition would you recommend, given the opportunity?

7.4.2 Evaluative questions about team selection (organizational)

The time required to develop a new system depends, in part, upon a team's ability to reach decisions rapidly on the many issues confronting it. Team members must have the authority to commit the resources of their respective organizations. If they do not, the timeliness of the process will be jeopardized.

Earlier we raised a question about who had the real knowledge and influence required to develop a utilitarian system — user or technician. What we will attempt to determine in this section is how much specific knowledge and influence do the team's technical and user participants possess.

By answering the following questions, you should gain insight into the quality of resources that your team has available to it through its membership.

☐ How does the team measure up in terms of

○ authority
○ influence
○ project knowledge

☐ What recent team problems, if any, might be explained by the fact that team members lacked authority to commit their respective departments?

☐ What recent team problems, if any, might be explained by the fact that team members lacked influence within the total organization?

☐ What recent team problems, if any, might be explained by the fact that members did not possess project-related skills and knowledge?

☐ If you had to replace an existing team member,

○ whom would you choose to replace and why?
○ what characteristics would you most like to see in the replacement and why?

7.4.3 Evaluative questions about team selection (group)

In addition to organizational factors that ought to influence team-member selections, there is a second set of criteria for assessing the team as a work group. In Chapter 1, I mentioned the expectation that the team would prove to be synergistic, exceeding what might have been accomplished on an individual basis. Obviously, the most basic requirement for a synergistic team is that the members be capable of working with reasonable harmony and common purpose.

In using the results of your analysis to answer the following questions, you will begin to evaluate your team and its potential for working together as a cohesive work group. You will also get a feel for some of the personal and emotional aspects of team performance, and thus begin to deal with the criticism that systems development is overly rational in its view of organizations.

☐ How does the team measure up in terms of

○ interpersonal skills
○ sharing team objectives
○ feelings about goal importance

☐ What recent team problems, if any, might be explained by the fact that the team members do not possess strong interpersonal skills?

☐ What recent team problems, if any, might be explained by the fact that the team members do not share common objectives?

☐ What recent team problems, if any, might be explained by the fact that the team members have other goals that they believe are more important than team goals?

☐ If you had to replace an existing team member on the basis of team considerations,

　　○ which team member would you choose to replace and why?

　　○ to which characteristics would you give greatest weight in selecting a replacement and why?

7.4.4 Evaluative questions about team selection (individual)

Let us return once again to the promise that teams would prove to be synergistic. Our review of the research literature has indicated that randomly selected teams do perform better than the "average" individual, but not better than the "best" individuals. Furthermore, we have discovered that both rational and emotional individual characteristics can be used to help identify the best individuals for the team. Thus, team synergism will increase as the quality of the individual team member is increased.

Working with your data analysis, you should answer the following set of evaluative questions. The answers that you provide will complete the third dimension to our team-selection criteria.

☐ How does the team measure up in terms of

　　○ general intelligence
　　○ dependability
　　○ social sensitivity
　　○ being well-adjusted

☐ What recent team problems, if any, might be explained by the fact that team member(s) did not demonstrate a high degree of intelligence?

☐ What recent team problems, if any, might be explained by the fact that a team member(s) is undependable?

☐ What recent team problems, if any, might be explained by the fact that a team member(s) is not socially sensitive toward other team members and external groups?

☐ What recent team problems, if any, might be explained by the fact that a team member(s) is not a well-adjusted individual?

☐ If you had to replace an existing team member on the basis of individual considerations,

    ○ which team member would you choose to replace and why?

    ○ what individual characteristics would you give the greatest weight to in selecting a replacement and why?

7.4.5 Evaluative questions about the team profile

In each of the preceding four evaluations, we focused on a single team dimension. If we are to obtain a satisfactory overall assessment of team strengths and weaknesses, we need to stand back for a moment to review the team profile for all characteristics.

The following series of evaluative questions is intended to facilitate your broader evaluation of the team's strengths and weaknesses.

☐ In what areas is the team membership strongest? weakest?

☐ Are there particular members whom you judge to be too weak on too many variables?

☐ Given the mix of existing strengths and weaknesses, what sorts of problems do you expect the team to be most susceptible to? Have there been recent problems and achievements that can be explained by the team profile?

☐ To what extent does the team profile reflect the characteristics of an autonomous work group?

☐ What do you recommend as a way of strengthening the team membership?

7.4.6 Evaluative questions about autonomous work groups

Where does the responsibility for project success or failure lie? If the systems development team is to be viewed as the focal point, then it must have the autonomy needed to control its own destiny. Many of the arguments presented in Part I about who ought to make systems development decisions — users or technicians — reflected a struggle for control over the development process. If either side were successful, it would serve to render the team to the status of an instrument to be directed and used by outside forces.

In this section, you will want to evaluate the extent to which your team is being permitted to function as a truly autonomous work group. By answering the following questions, you should obtain valuable insights into these matters.

- ☐ How autonomous is the team with regard to performing its task? What specific recommendations could you make to increase task autonomy?

- ☐ How autonomous is the team with regard to skills and abilities? What specific recommendations could you make to increase autonomy in skills and abilities?

- ☐ How autonomous is the team with regard to decision-making? What specific recommendations could you make to increase decision-making autonomy?

- ☐ How autonomous is the team with regard to reward systems? What specific recommendations could you make to increase reward-system autonomy?

- ☐ What areas do you feel are in greatest need of actions to increase autonomy? Why?

7.5 Practical suggestions

Recent systems development efforts have been characterized by over-compensation for those early days when users were not invited to participate actively. One visible outcome of this need to over-compensate has been the creation of relatively large user committees. If you find through your analysis and evaluation that this has occurred, it may be helpful if you can encourage an alternate strategy that necessitates a small core of full-time participants, and permits others to participate on a part-time basis. However, the strategy will be only marginally successful unless it also carries an endorsement that clearly places the management and decision-making responsibilities within the jurisdiction of the full-time membership the team. For this reason, full-time team members must be carefully selected.

Naturally, it is always possible that the final team selection will result in a less than ideal membership. In some instances, actions other than a change in membership can be taken to assist in rectifying the problem. For example, if the team members are found to be deficient on the basis of organizational factors (authority, influence, project knowledge), a strategy can be developed to increase part-time participation by people within the organization who do meet the necessary criteria. Also, specialized training can be sought for team members in an effort to increase their knowledge in certain project-related areas. Interpersonal skills can be developed through proper training. Many workshops held around the country every year offer people the opportunity to gain these skills. Consultants as well can help team members to address these problems.

Individual team members will possess a variety of strengths and weaknesses, and members should be encouraged to work with one another in mutually complementary ways.

Team-member selection is one crucial factor determining the team's effectiveness. A second important factor is autonomy, for without some degree of autonomy, the systems development team will not be able to develop into a highly effective and cohesive work group. In effect, it will become simply another candidate to blame for eventual failure. One can expect to experience considerable difficulty in convincing an organization to provide greater autonomy to the team. To some extent, it is important to demonstrate to management that the team will not become so autonomous that it will create its own goals and objectives in conflict with prevailing management goals and objectives. Care will need to be taken to insure that formal links exist between the team and those who stand to benefit or lose from its work.

Chapter 7: References

1. J.R. Hackman, "Work Design," *Improving Life at Work,* eds. J.R. Hackman and J.L. Suttle (Santa Monica, Calif.: Goodyear Publishing, 1977), pp. 3, 96−162.

2. E.F. Harrison, *The Managerial Decision-Making Process* (Boston: Houghton-Mifflin, 1975), pp. 189−91.

3. F.P. Brooks, Jr., *The Mythical Man-Month* (Reading, Mass.: Addison-Wesley, 1975).

4. D. Marquis, "Ways of Organizing Projects," *Innovation,* Vol. 5 (1969), pp. 25−33.

5. J.R. Galbraith, *Organization Design* (Reading, Mass.: Addison-Wesley, 1977), pp. 120−22.

6. E.F. Harrison, op. cit., pp. 195−98.

7. M.E. Shaw, *Group Dynamics* (New York: McGraw-Hill, 1976), pp. 189−92.

Social Structure and Interaction | 8

Bringing a group of people together and designating them a "systems development team" obviously does not make them a team. Even when a great deal of care has been taken in the selection of team members, the result will not be an effective team unless the members view themselves, and are viewed by others, as integral members of the team, each with a significant role or function to perform. There is ample evidence to support the statement that data processing, user, and management personnel have not traditionally worked well together even when they have attempted to employ team approaches. This is, in part, attributable to the fact that they have approached their relationship almost totally as a formal way of dealing with a specific set of tasks. In so doing, they have ignored the more subtle, informal aspects of social structure and interaction.

In this chapter, we will focus on the team as a social entity, in which members have specific roles, status, and power. Also, we shall note how the team as a small group creates norms, develops cohesiveness or experiences conflict, and functions within the broader context of reward systems. In this way, we will begin to note how a team develops into a cohesive, autonomous unit that functions, in part, to maintain itself as a team. These maintenance functions are important to overall team effectiveness. If a team experiences problems, such as a high degree of internal conflict, it will not be able to work effectively on task-oriented goals.

8.1 Role, status, and power

For a systems development team, we would hope to see all members (technicians, users, and managers) playing a significant role. Also, we would like to think that each member will find it possible to acquire a measure of additional status and influence by working with the team. Thus, in toto, we would like to think that participation as a team member can be overwhelmingly positive and satisfying. Experience to date would indicate that it is difficult, in practice, to achieve this very ideal outcome. Understanding the social structure of the team in terms of individual roles, status, and power can be helpful in attempting to isolate and address some of the problems that are interfering with attainment of the ideal.

The members of a systems development team may have other commitments external to the team. For example, a team representative from the accounting office may also have continuing duties and responsibilities within that office. This splitting of responsibilities can (but need not) cause a member to view himself as being only peripherally committed to the team. There are other possible negative consequences resulting from this sort of role-splitting. First, other team members may view that individual's commitment to the team as secondary and thus of little importance to them. Second, there may be times when the two roles come into direct conflict. For example, a team position on an issue may be at odds with the position taken by the individual's supervisor. As Wexley and Yukl have pointed out, this sort of role conflict can cause a person to become upset or frustrated.[1] The net effect of any of these role problems will be to inhibit the team from functioning with optimal effectiveness.

Another dimension of roles should be mentioned briefly: There may be a discrepancy between how a particular team member perceives his role and what other team members expect. This sort of discrepancy can lead to considerable conflict within the team, resulting in a loss of effectiveness.

A second important aspect of a team's social structure is status. As Shaw has pointed out, there is a significant and frequently overlooked difference between "position" and "status."[2] While an individual may occupy a position, such as team leader, the evaluation of that position by all of the team members is what determines its status. Understanding status differences will help to clarify communications patterns within the team, as well as individual job satisfaction or dissatisfaction. Members with high status are the key elements in the team's communications network. Also, we would expect to find a correlation between high status and the sense that the job being done is both important and satisfying.

Some team members have more power than others; they are more able to influence others and less likely to be influenced by others. Of course, which team member has the most power may be situational, in the sense that a member may have more power in one area (for example, database design) and less in another (such as office procedure). Remembering from Chapters 2 and 4 some of the rather forceful statements made by practitioners about decision-makers, we must examine a team's power structure to see who really influences what decisions, and to be assured that those exercising power also meet other criteria, such as having special knowledge and skill related to the problem.

8.2 Cohesive teams

Group cohesiveness is a fundamentally important topic in any discussion of teams. Since the Hawthorne Studies,* it has been apparent that some groups can achieve goals despite serious obstacles, and one plausible explanation for this is group cohesiveness.[3] Since most large-scale systems projects have numerous pitfalls, the potential positive consequences of team cohesiveness are of special interest to us. Shepherd has described cohesion as composed of five forces that serve to bind members of a group to one another and to the group as a whole:

- the satisfaction that members obtain from being in a group
- the degree of closeness and warmth that group members feel for each other
- the pride felt by members as a result of their being in a group
- the ability of members to meet crises confronting them as a group
- the willingness of members of a group to be frank and honest in their expression of ideas and feelings[4]

With regard to systems development teams, we should not be hasty in assuming that a high quality, broadly acceptable product will be produced more quickly simply because a group is cohesive. Shaw suggests that highly cohesive groups are more effective in achieving whatever goals the members establish, but notes that these may not be the same goals that others would like them to achieve.[5] Thus, from our point of view, it is important to ascertain both the degree of team cohesiveness and the degree to which the goals of the development team are consistent with those of the larger organization.

As people develop into cohesive teams, they create a set of formal and informal rules about what constitutes proper and improper

---

*These Studies were conducted from 1924 to 1927 because of AT&T management's interest in increasing productivity, and were named for the Western Electric plant where they took place. In the Studies, researchers experimented with such environmental conditions as lighting to discover the effect on worker productivity.

behavior. These norms are powerful, creating an environment in which team members can expect some degree of consistency in the behavior of individual team members. They also establish criteria for individual praise and sanction within the team. Thus, in a positive sense, one would hope that a team might develop its own formal and informal rules that stress the need for dependability, cooperativeness, timeliness, and so on.

As Lawler has pointed out, both intrinsic and extrinsic rewards are powerful and important determinants of human behavior.[6] Being a member of a cohesive team can be a rewarding job experience in and of itself. Also, the reward mechanisms employed by an organization may encourage or discourage team cohesiveness. For example, if the organization rewards team members based upon individual performance, it will discourage team cohesiveness; if it rewards the team members based upon team performance, it will encourage cohesiveness.

The effective team will be one in which the membership and the organization have successfully dealt with each of the above issues. Conversely, the team will be ineffective and have difficulty in focusing upon the specific development task if it is bogged down in conflict and its members are working at cross purposes.

8.3 Team analysis: social structure and interaction

The effectiveness of team-member interactions, both internal and external, is critical to the team's ability to work cooperatively in developing a new system. However, this dimension of a team's performance is often overlooked. The results are evidenced in numerous projects in which after literally years of debate there is still no fundamental agreement on the new system's purpose, let alone a tangible, working product.

If we are to avoid the numerous errors of the past, we will need to focus more clearly upon the social structure and interaction aspects of team performance. An analysis of these factors can help us to determine which members of the team truly participate and which have the greatest decision-making influence. We will also be able to determine the extent to which the group functions as a true team, as opposed to simply a collection of individuals.

Once again, you will perform a series of data collection and analysis activities for the team with which you have been working. The guidelines center on six objectives.

First, you will gather some very specific information about each team member's role. Second, you will determine how each role is viewed by all of the team members. Third, you will relate data collected on the physical environment to each team member's role, status, and power (or influence). Fourth, you will attempt to assess team members' satisfaction and team cohesiveness. Next, you will identify the team's formal and informal rules and enforcement tactics. Finally, you will gain insight into the team's reward mechanisms.

8.3.1 Data collection

Step 1: Gather some basic information about each team member's role.

- ☐ Describe his role as each member perceives it. If his role has a formal title, such as data librarian, so indicate. If the member feels his role is ambiguous, so indicate.

- ☐ Describe each participant's role as it is perceived by the other team members.

- ☐ Identify external roles for each team member whose involvement is split between the team and some other functional area.

- ☐ When multiple roles are involved, identify which one the team member feels is primary.

- ☐ Ask the team members to recall instances of conflicts between their team role and another role. How did they deal with the problem?

Step 2: Assess the status associated with each role by asking for each team member's perceptions.

- ☐ Ask each member to rate (on a scale from 1 = low to 5 = high) the various team positions in terms of the prestige associated with them (include a ranking for his own position).

Team Position	Individual Raters					
	*					

*Place the rater's initials in the boxes on this line and the respective ratings below.

☐ Develop a version of the chart to include a single composite score for each position.

Step 3: Review previous information you have obtained.

☐ From Chapter 6 on the physical environment, what data analyzed in Step 2 is relevant to the current discussions on status?

☐ From Chapter 6, again, what data analyzed in Step 3 is relevant to the current discussions on power or influence?

Step 4: Ask each team member to respond to the following statements with the code: (1) strongly agree, (2) agree, (3) neutral, (4) disagree, or (5) strongly disagree.

☐ I personally derive a great deal of satisfaction from working with this team.

☐ I feel that our team is a close working group in which people care about one another.

☐ I am personally proud of my work with this group.

☐ When there is a crisis, we are usually able to meet the challenge as a group.

☐ I feel that it is possible to be frank and honest in exchanges with other team members.

Summarize the responses so that there is a single composite score for each item.

Step 5: Ask the members of the team to list the following:

☐ formal and informal rules or expectations that the team members have of one another

☐ actions that would cause the other team members to praise the individual

☐ actions that would result in negative statements or feelings by other team members

Step 6: Based upon observation and discussion with team members, determine the relative frequency of each of the following types of reward (rate on a scale of 1 to 5, 1 meaning very frequently, and 5 for infrequently or not all):

☐ The duties themselves are rewarding.

☐ Working with the other team members is a rewarding experience.

☐ Members of the team receive individual rewards and/or praise from external sources based upon individual accomplishment.

☐ Team members receive rewards and/or praise as a team from external sources based upon team accomplishments.

8.4 Evaluation of the analysis: social structure and interaction

The data collected and analyzed in the previous section continues to point to some of the less visible but extremely powerful determinants of team effectiveness.

We can, for purposes of discussion, broadly categorize the activities of the team as being either task-related or maintenance-related. The specific job of systems design is an example of a task-related activity. In the forthcoming evaluation, we will focus primarily on maintenance-related team activities. Whenever a team spends time discussing difficulties that its members are having in their interactions with one another or with other people, it is spending time on team maintenance. In this way, the team is dealing with issues that could generate conflict and an adversarial climate, which would prevent the team from focusing on task-related activities. Furthermore, team-maintenance activities can lead to very positive consequences such as greater team cohesiveness.

To the extent possible, we will continue to relate evaluation materials to the systems development problems cited in Part I.

8.4.1 Evaluative questions about roles

We frequently find that all team members do not participate equally in a development project. In particular, data processing people have been accused of dominating the decision-making process for new systems. From their own perspective, data processing people sometimes feel that while management and users talk about the need for participation, they are two groups largely unwilling or unable to make the degree of commitment necessary.

In our brief review of the relevant research literature, it became clear that, whenever people have multiple roles, conflict may arise between those roles. Naturally, this can create problems for the individual team member and thus affect overall team effectiveness.

A second area that needs to be evaluated concerns the extent to which any particular role is clearly understood by all participants. Thus, if one individual is to be the final authority on database structure, the legitimacy of that role needs to be supported by the entire team.

The following questions seek to assist you in evaluating individual roles as they influence the team with which you have been working.

☐ Do members of the team have specific and meaningful roles?

☐ Is there consistency between individual and team perceptions about each person's role?

☐ How would you evaluate the importance of team roles versus external roles that the team members hold?

☐ Are frequent role conflicts experienced by team members?

☐ What negative consequences can you identify that may have resulted from

   ○ role ambiguity or differences in role perception
   ○ multiple roles or role conflicts

8.4.2 *Evaluative questions about status*

For those participating in development of a new system, there is frequently much more involved than the task of intellectually solving the technical riddle at hand. Emotional factors are also involved and become far more apparent when we consider characteristics such as status. The desirability of being a member of a particular team or of holding a particular position on that team will be influenced by the prestige associated with that membership or that position.

We have previously indicated that development of a new system is a complex task requiring the dedication of the very best people from within the organization. Clearly, one cannot hope to attract such highly talented people if there are none of the emotional but very practical advantages of status associated with work on the development team.

Answering the following evaluative questions will provide further insight into status and its relationships to other team characteristics.

☐ Which positions have the most/least prestige associated with them?

☐ How does the data on prestige relate to previously collected data about intrateam communications patterns?

☐ What level of prestige do you find associated with each ambiguous role?

☐ Reviewing the team-selection criteria used in the preceding chapter (team size, use of both full-time and part-time participants, and heterogeneity), what relationships, if any, can you see between status and those factors?

8.4.3 Evaluative questions about power

The large-scale use of computing in most business organizations has evolved to the point at which decisions about new systems can have a profound and lasting impact on the organization. Because of this, it is important for us to understand who within the team framework has power or influence on the team's decision-making processes.

We also need to examine how power or influence can affect the basic communications structure of the team by making it more centralized. The following evaluative questions are aimed at providing greater insight into power as it relates to team structure and interaction.

☐ Who are the most influential team members?

☐ Is there any relationship between influence and communications patterns?

☐ Is there any relationship between people with influence and those with prestige?

☐ Is there a relationship between people with influence and those who best meet the criteria for selection as a team member?

8.4.4 Evaluative questions about team cohesiveness

As previously stated, becoming a synergistic systems development team requires achieving team cohesiveness. We have also indicated that it is important to maintain consistency between the goals of the cohesive team and the goals of the larger organization. Many of the failures of new systems development can be attributed to the energetic and effective development of systems that are neither needed nor wanted by the organization.

Using the available data, you should attempt to provide answers to the following evaluative questions. In so doing, you will gain further insight into the cohesiveness of your team, as well as into the degree of consistency between its goals and those of the larger organization.

☐ In general, how would you evaluate the extent of team cohesiveness?

☐ Are there members of the team who do not share in the feeling of cohesiveness?

☐ Can you give reasons that might substantiate why an individual(s) is more peripheral to the functioning of the team? (Suggestion: Review data collected on the individual team members in each of the previous chapters in Part II.)

☐ What team problems, if any, would you judge to have occurred as a result of the team's being a cohesive entity whose goals and objectives were different from organizational expectations?

☐ What possible actions can you envision for improving team cohesiveness?

☐ What possible actions can you envision for bringing team and organizational expectations into greater harmony?

8.4.5 Evaluative questions about group norms

Up to this point, we have not said a great deal about conformity. And yet, when we talk about group norms, we are, in effect, focusing on individuals conforming to a set of rules established by the team members themselves. We are also referring to the group pressures that can be used to encourage conformity.

From our vantage point, it is more or less accepted that effective team performance requires some norming or conformity to group goals and processes. What is of direct concern, and as yet unanswered, is whether the team norms aid in developing a large-scale information system. Naturally, a set of norms that supports systems development would be preferable to another set of norms, such as one that simply encouraged a lot of debate over a period of years.

Using the available data, you should answer the following evaluative questions about team norms.

☐ Are the team norms supportive of developing a large-scale information system in a timely fashion? Explain.

☐ Does the team enforce its norms with praise or sanction?

8.4.6 Evaluative questions about team rewards

The reward system within which a team operates is a most powerful determinant affecting job satisfaction, team cohesiveness, and relationships with external groups. Historically, data processing people have been rewarded for keeping technologically current, while users have been rewarded on an equally narrow basis within their functional area. In applying team approaches to the development of large-scale information systems, we may discover that the team approach clashes with the existing reward mechanisms. We may also find that the team requires a somewhat different reward system than that used when the focal point is the productive individual.

The following questions offer some guidance in evaluating the appropriateness of the reward system within which the team operates.

☐ What is the most frequent form of reward used?

☐ What form of reward is most infrequently used?

☐ What conclusions might you draw about the relationship between the reward system employed and

   ○ job satisfaction
   ○ team cohesiveness
   ○ team relationships with other groups

☐ Are there specific team problems that in your judgment reflect the inappropriateness of the existing reward system? Describe those problems.

☐ What changes, if any, to the reward system do you recommend?

8.5 Practical suggestions

If a team is to be effective, its members must be free to participate fully in the activities of the team. Full commitment to the goals and objectives of the team is essential and is to be expected from each team member. A minimal initial commitment rarely will change into a major commitment of its own accord over time. In fact, the reverse is usually the case: A team member with a minimal initial commitment frequently ceases to participate at all when the demands of the project increase. In addition, the role and commitment level of each team member must be made explicit to all other members of the team and to external groups and individuals.

The status associated with being a member of a systems development team can be an inducement (or a dissuader) in attracting the best people to work on the team. If the analysis and evaluation of your team indicates that little status is associated with being a team member, it may be possible to develop a strategy that will increase the overall status associated with team membership or particular team roles. For example, establishing direct lines of communication between the team and top management affords a degree of visibility to the team. Also, some role redefinition to include additional duties and responsibilities may be useful in improving people's perceptions about the status attached to a position.

Power is something that everyone agrees exists and most people feel they can recognize. Nevertheless, people agree power is difficult to define with precision, and thus almost impossible to measure with any degree of objectivity. For these reasons, you should take special care to remember that your assessments about power or influence are highly subjective. Nonetheless, if you determine that the person(s) exerting the most influence is not the individual who best meets the criteria for team membership, this may signal that resulting team decisions need to be closely scrutinized for accuracy and quality.

A major objective in team development is to create an environment that will simultaneously result in team cohesiveness and harmony between team and organizational goals and expectations. When a team does not display cohesiveness, common recommendations include

- to encourage it to spend greater amounts of time on group maintenance activities
- to identify (or assign) a group process facilitator who will work with the team in achieving greater cohesiveness
- to hold special team-building and similar training sessions (frequently at a location away from the job)

Because teams may experience difficulty in achieving the desired level of cohesiveness, it is best if an organization invests in team-development activities when the team is formed. This permits the team to start its task-oriented work with a measure of cohesiveness.

In order for the team to achieve its goal within a reasonable time, its members must perform according to a set of norms that is supportive of the systems development process. In a sense, norms represent the internal reward system. External rewards may be used to change those norms that are not supportive of new systems development.

At times, people have difficulty accepting the concept of group rewards, since they see it as a direct threat to the cherished notion of "rugged individualism." The argument has no credibility at all if one considers the following:

- The magnitude of large-scale systems development exceeds the capabilities of an individual and, therefore, requires the cooperative effort of many people.

- Groups of individuals create their own norms (conform) in ways that may or may not be consistent with individual needs and expectations. Groups reward and sanction their members individually based upon these group norms.

- By creating group versus individual rewards, management permits the group greater autonomy and flexibility in its treatment of individuals, but holds it accountable as an entity.

For example, there is nothing in the team-reward concept to prohibit management from establishing a graduated scale for pay bonuses at the team level based upon team achievement; and also allow for the group to redistribute its total "bonus" in unequal pieces to individual team members based upon perceived individual merit. Beyond this, it is frequently difficult in large organizations for most people to receive individual praise and acknowledgment from busy supervisors. Within the team, the likelihood of obtaining more or less immediate recognition for good work and good effort from other team members is very high indeed. To some extent, being a member of a team will probably permit each member to be part of a more significant contribution than that achieved individually. While members have to share the resulting recognition with others, their sense of achievement remains highly individualized.

Chapter 8: References

1. K.N. Wexley and G.A. Yukl, *Organizational Behavior and Personnel Psychology* (Homewood, Ill.: Richard D. Irwin, Inc., 1977).

2. M.E. Shaw, *Group Dynamics* (New York: McGraw-Hill, 1976), p. 245.

3. F.J. Roethlisberger and W.J. Dickson, *Management and the Worker* (Cambridge, Mass.: Harvard University Press, 1947).

4. C.R. Shepherd, *Small Groups: Some Sociological Perspectives* (Scranton, Pa.: Chandler, 1964), p. 25.

5. M.E. Shaw, op. cit., p. 234.

6. E.E. Lawler, III, "Reward Systems," *Improving Life at Work,* eds. J.R. Hackman and J.L. Suttle, (Santa Monica, Calif.: Goodyear Publishing, 1977), pp. 4, 163–226.

Task Environment and Leadership | 9

As stated before, one of the factors that most clearly differentiates a systems development team from other kinds of small work groups is that it is very task-oriented. The task of systems development is product-oriented, extremely complex, multidimensional, and highly uncertain. These four characteristics contribute to the uniqueness of the systems development environment.

The environment determines the type of leadership style that is most effective; that is, leadership is situationally dependent, as Fiedler and Chemers have pointed out.[1] Therefore, the individual who is a successful leader in other situations may or may not prove to be an effective systems development team leader. In the following sections, we will examine more closely both the systems development task environment and the leadership styles that appear to be most closely suited to the needs of that environment.

9.1 Task environment

The systems development task environment imposes significant constraints that need to be fully understood by the team, and for which the team must develop an effective plan of action. For these reasons, each of the above four characteristics of the task environment will be discussed below.

The purpose of a systems development team is to produce an effective new system. This purpose has a sort of ultimate priority, and other outcomes are clearly peripheral. It serves both as a "bottom-line" basis for determining success or failure, and as the primary criterion for reward. In attempting to achieve its goal, the team is further constrained by the limitations of time and the total resources available to it. Thus, the effective management of time and resources is crucial to the team's success.

The development of an effective information system is an extremely complex matter. It is unlikely that an organization will already include an individual or group of individuals who possess all of the knowledge and skills needed to develop the system. Hence, the systems development team will probably (in the ideal sense) consist of individuals who have very different knowledge and abilities, but who also possess skills for solving unique or novel problems. In the course of systems development, the team will need to acquire additional information to make (and remake) numerous decisions as needed.

The scope of a large-scale systems development effort is multidimensional, affecting many components of the total organization. By examining its relationships to the various functional departments and management, we can begin to appreciate why the use of a cross-functional team approach makes more sense than simply having one or a group of technicians handle the development.

Galbraith has suggested that the degree of certainty associated with a task is important in making an assessment of the task environment.[2] Using this approach, one would have to typify the task of systems development as being highly uncertain at the onset. That is, while the team knows its task — for example, to develop a personnel system — it does not possess at the onset all of the information needed to do its job. As progress is made in the actual development, uncertainty diminishes somewhat; but until the system is successfully implemented, there will be a continuing atmosphere of fundamental uncertainty.

In constructing a team to develop a complex, multidimensional product for which there are no all-knowing experts, we are implementing a new kind of organizational entity. We would expect that, if the team is successful, it will become the repository of knowledge about the system and, hence, most informed and best able to make decisions. The issue of team leadership becomes a critical one here not only in terms of how the team functions within itself, but also in terms of how the team performs in its obviously delicate relationships with both management and the functional organization.

9.2 Leadership style

Galbraith points out that there are two major qualities characterizing good leadership:

- ability to provide direction or structure, called by Galbraith initiating-structure behavior (that is, actions that impose structure on a project, such as assigning tasks to specific members or scheduling jobs)

- ability to provide support or consideration (that is, behavior expressing warmth and concern with respect to subordinates)[3]

In addition, Galbraith suggests that the influence that a leader has outside of the immediate work group and, in particular, higher in the organization, may be an important factor determining the leader's ability to influence subordinates.

There is some evidence that effective leadership style is contingent upon a number of task-related activities. For systems development teams, the following observations seem to be true regarding effective leadership:

- strong initiating-structure behaviors are generally important to team members, given the ambiguity and uncertainty of systems development

- considerate behavior is particularly important during those times in the project when subordinates are experiencing dissatisfaction with the work. Also, consideration can be a powerful reward mechanism if it is granted on the basis of genuine merit during these times of dissatisfaction.

- outside influence can affect the extent to which considerate behavior by a leader will affect subordinates. The systems development project apparently benefits from having a team leader with considerable external influence.

You will recall from Chapter 1 that, historically, technical expertise has been the primary basis upon which team or project leaders were selected. The observations stated above challenge that practice and suggest quite a different set of criteria for selection:

- task/project management skill
- external (organizational) influence
- considerate leadership

The degree of importance of each of the above criteria will vary with the task environment. For example, during periods of extreme uncertainty, a leader who has extraordinary task-management skill would be more desirable. During those times when there is conflict and turmoil within the team (or in its interactions with external groups), the considerate leader who is also viewed as having organizational influence may be most desirable.

9.3 Team analysis: task environment and leadership

Analyzing the task environment and leadership style associated with a team is a complex and revealing activity. The problem is compounded if the formal leader is not the true leader. Our primary focus in the subsequent analysis will be on the true team leader, while noting what leadership functions, if any, are performed by the formal leader.

In the data collection and analysis exercises that follow, we will seek first to gain insight into the extent to which task uncertainty exists as a function of systems development. Here, we will be quite specific in delineating the kinds of uncertainty that exist. Second, we will assess the extent to which effective team leadership is being practiced.

9.3.1 Data collection

Step 1: Based upon knowledge gained about this project and the people involved in it (supplemented by any additional information you wish to obtain at this time), do the following:

☐ Outline the goals of the project in some detail.

☐ Identify which goals are new and/or experimental to the total organization.

☐ Identify which goals are new and/or experimental to members of the team.

☐ Determine how the goals were set.

Step 2: Analyze the new system's requirements from a purely technical/computing perspective. Will the new system require

☐ computer hardware that is new to the organization? to the project team members?

☐ computer software or software techniques that are new to the organization? to the project team members?

Step 3: Analyze the new system's requirements from a business perspective. Will the new system require

☐ changes in the ways in which people do work and/or the skills they need to do the job?

☐ changes in the people with whom individuals work, and consequently with their working relationships?

☐ changes in the number of people who will do the work and/or to whom they report in the hierarchy?

Step 4: Working with the team leader and subordinates, describe the task/project management system employed, including the following:

- ☐ job scheduling (including job estimation)
- ☐ task assignment
- ☐ status reporting
- ☐ employee evaluation criteria and procedure
- ☐ decision-making methods employed (refer to Section 4.2)

Step 5: Based upon your prior analyses as well as any additional information you have been able to obtain, do the following:

- ☐ Evaluate the extent of influence that the team leader has on groups and individuals external to the group.
- ☐ Evaluate the extent to which other team members have a greater or lesser degree of external influence than the team leader.

Step 6: Based upon your prior observations and analyses, as well as any additional findings you wish to obtain, make the following judgments:

- ☐ Assess the extent to which the leader is viewed, and views himself, as a warm and understanding leader.
- ☐ Determine the extent to which the leader's considerate behavior is tied to effective performance by individuals.
- ☐ Assess the extent to which considerate behavior by the leader is seen to increase during periods of frustration and disillusionment.
- ☐ State the extent to which team members value considerate behavior by the leader as both significant and personally rewarding.

9.4 Evaluation of the analysis: task environment and leadership

Recall that, in Chapter 1, we stated that the failure of systems development projects relate to three issues: management skill and involvement, formal versus informal process, and technical and organizational incompatibility. We also said these issues share a common focus upon individual and group interaction as the reason for systems development problems.

Now, we are in a position to raise a number of evaluative questions to identify the potentially troublesome interactions for your team. Specifically, for each of the six steps in the analysis of the preceding section, a brief description of the ideal team model introduces a set of evaluative questions. The first three sets focus on assessing the degree of uncertainty associated with a systems development task. The latter three involve criteria for effective leadership. You should utilize the data collected in this chapter's analysis plus the relevant data obtained in the prior analyses to answer the questions.

9.4.1 Evaluative questions about uncertainty in project goals

You will recall that sharing of common goals is one of the distinguishing characteristics of a true team. Naturally, if a team is to share in common goals, the goals must be clearly stated and the team members must feel comfortable with them. We might even expect that the members would have played a key role in their development.

You should consider asking the following evaluative questions as a test of the extent to which your team conforms to the ideal model.

☐ Have the goals previously been clearly stated in some detail and shared with all team members?

☐ If the project contains many features that are new and/or experimental to the organization, what steps are being taken to prepare for the eventual change? What additional suggestions do you have (such as special training programs)?

☐ If the project contains many features that are new and/or experimental to the team, what steps have been taken to prepare the team members? What additional suggestions do you have?

☐ In general, how would you evaluate the degree of uncertainty felt by members and the program established to deal with it?

☐ To what extent did the team members play a role in the development of these goals? Do they share in the belief that the goals are important?

9.4.2 Evaluative questions about technical uncertainty

We mentioned earlier that there are times when the new computer technology will clash with the existing organizational structure, or prove to be beyond the current skill levels of the data processing staff. If we are to be prepared for these eventualities, then it is necessary to minimize the potential negative consequences for both the technical and non-technical staffs by developing a specific plan of action.

The following evaluative questions attempt to determine the extent to which the team has anticipated the problems associated with the introduction of new technology.

- ☐ What steps are being taken to reduce the degree of uncertainty associated with new computer hardware (in both the team and the total organization)? What additional suggestions do you have?

- ☐ What steps are being taken to reduce the degree of uncertainty associated with new computer software and/or software techniques (in both the team and the total organization)? What additional suggestions do you have?

9.4.3 Evaluative questions about procedural uncertainty

Just as there was concern about the introduction of new computing hardware and software, the team should be concerned about the business procedures and practices that will be introduced by the new system.

Much of what we refer to as user resistance and dissatisfaction result from suddenly springing vast changes in procedure on users at the time of systems delivery. Uncertainty about how the new system will affect existing office procedure also makes it difficult for users to evaluate positively or to encourage the systems development process.

Through the following questions, we will evaluate the extent to which the team has been effective in informing others of proposed procedural change and in planning specific actions to ensure a smooth transition to using the new procedures.

- ☐ Do people within and external to the team have a clear understanding of how the new system will affect those who will be required to operate or use it?

- ☐ Do people external to the team feel comfortable with proposed changes in staffing and reporting structures?

☐ What steps have been taken or are being planned to ensure that transition to a new system is a smooth and positive experience? What additional suggestions do you have?

☐ How effective a job has the team done in recognizing the uncertainty associated with its work and in constructing a plan for reducing uncertainty as development of the system progresses?

9.4.4 Evaluative questions about task/project management skill

Effective task and project management are in large part the responsibility of the team leader. However, in the systems development team environment, it is important that the team leader utilize the team's breadth of skills and capabilities for evaluating individual performance and for decision-making. None of the team members is all-knowing, including the team leader.

The following questions are designed to enable us to evaluate the extent to which there is a rational plan for team management that includes the active participation of all members.

☐ What aspects of task/project management need greater definition?

☐ To what extent, if at all, are task assignments and time/resource estimates made with input from the team member(s) who must perform the work?

☐ To what extent does the leader hold individual members accountable to the team? (For example, are team members asked to critique one another's work?)

☐ To what extent does the leader employ decision-making processes to maximize the potential for creative contributions by all team members?

☐ To what extent does the leader support an approach to decision-making that recognizes the need for data collection and aggregation prior to the act of deciding (refer to Section 4.2)?

☐ What suggestions would you make to the team leader that would assist in managing other people's work?

9.4.5 Evaluative questions about external influence

External influence is an important factor in determining effective leadership. It is a second criterion by which subordinates evaluate their leadership, and it is also a factor in determining how others will perceive the team. In some respects, a study of the external influence that members of a team possess is also a study in informal leadership within the team.

The following questions seek to identify who, if anyone, on the team possesses this vital ingredient.

☐ If the only measure of effective leadership was external influence, how would you rank the current leader? Who on the team would be potentially the most effective leader?

☐ What conclusions might you draw when one or more of the team members has more external leverage than the team leader? What potential problems might you expect if this were the situation?

9.4.6 Evaluative questions about considerate leadership

Considerate behavior represents our third criterion for effective leadership. A leader's feeling about his degree of consideration may be quite different from the other team members' perceptions of his considerate behavior. Also, the value of considerate behavior may be tied to the discretion with which it is employed, and to the leader's influence outside of the team, particularly with management.

The following questions have been constructed to provide greater insight into this third aspect of team leadership. At the conclusion, we should be able to evaluate the current leadership on the basis of a set of criteria far more appropriate than the criterion of technical expertise.

☐ Are there discrepancies between the leader's self-assessment and the team's assessment of the degree of considerate leadership being exercised?

☐ Is the leader utilizing considerate behavior as an effective reward and coaching mechanism? (Please explain your answer.)

☐ Is there any correlation between the leader's degree of external influence and the perceived value of his consideration?

□ If a team included different people with the needed leadership credentials but no one person with all of them, what sort of organizational structure might you suggest? How would it work?

9.5 Practical suggestions

Not all leadership styles will be equally effective in a particular task environment. Therefore, clearly understanding the nature of the systems development environment is an important prerequisite to selecting a leadership style that will be maximally effective.

Uncertainty in project goals creates major problems within the project team. A leadership style that encourages team members to participate in goal development appears to have several distinct advantages: First, it raises questions early in the project about the feasibility of the goals. Second, it encourages early identification of areas in which team members require additional training and skill-building. Finally, it facilitates internalization of the goals by the team members.

Technical and procedural uncertainties represent areas that can affect the team in its relationship with others as well as within itself. A highly active leadership style is needed to identify clearly all of the potential problem areas, and to create a detailed plan for obtaining the answers, the training resources, and the time required to begin reducing the uncertainty associated with these aspects of the project. Whenever proposed changes can potentially affect other groups, a strategy will be required to bring those groups into the decision-making process.

Project- and task-management skill should not be confused with authoritarian rule; it is possible for all members to participate in the development of job schedules and time estimates. However, it is a unique set of leadership skills that permits a person to bring ideas and suggestions together into a workable schedule, execute it, and monitor progress. If no one on the team possesses these skills, it will be absolutely essential either to train one of the team members or to augment the team. To do otherwise will result in large-scale confusion and subsequent failure.

Individuals who are high on the initiating-structure behavior scale are sometimes low on the consideration scale. Considerate leadership from a person recognized as having strong external influence may be particularly important when team members are experiencing disappointment, dissatisfaction, or frustration with the work. During such times, the team and the team leader may be responsive to a more extensive involvement by top management, with the explicit purpose of providing some influential consideration during these difficult times.

The decision-making process is central to the efficiency and effectiveness with which a team functions. Many times, a team's problems with decision-making reflect a lack of understanding about group versus individual decisions. In such cases, a sharing of materials described in Chapter 4 may be appropriate and helpful.

If the team is not effectively dealing with the above issues, then it is heading on a disastrous course. Often, the individual designated as a team leader is not the best-equipped member of the team to deal with all of these issues. One of the advantages of the team approach is that it lends itself to having many true leaders, depending upon the particular needs of the situation. If a team is experiencing problems of this nature, a strategy is required that will permit the team to identify the best person available to meet the particular challenges of the moment. The chances that this will happen successfully relate to the team's communications and authority structure. If there is a highly centralized communications structure, the formal team leader may find such a move to be threatening. On the other hand, a decentralized structure would tend to find this situational delegation of leadership authority to be quite natural.

Chapter 9: References

1. F.E. Fiedler and M.M. Chemers, *Leadership and Effective Management* (Glenview, Ill.: Scott, Foresman & Co., 1974), pp. 56-72.

2. J.R. Galbraith, *Organization Design* (Reading, Mass.: Addison-Wesley, 1977), pp. 35-39.

3. Ibid., pp. 315-23.

Epilogue
Teams — Past, Present, and Future

"So we find that . . . without exception the amenities and refinements of life . . . all were taught gradually by usage and the active mind's experience as men groped their way forward step by step. So each particular development is brought gradually to the fore by the advance of time, and reason lifts it into the light of day. Men saw one notion after another take shape within their minds until by their arts they scaled the topmost peak."

— Titus Lucretius Carus
The Nature of the Universe, approx. 55 B.C.

The advent of large-scale database systems and the growing awareness of problems in the relationships between systems, user, and management personnel have created an environment in which people have become responsive to the concept of applying team approaches to information systems development. In many instances, this realization has preceded a thorough understanding of the requirements for effective team performance. Thus, the reviews of early team approaches were varied — some proclaiming tremendous success, some admitting disappointment. On balance, the degree of success proved sufficient to spur a growing interest in using teams, and in analyzing the reasons for team success and team failure.

For this reason, practitioners of the team approach have reviewed the research findings of social scientists and organizational specialists for relevance to systems development teams. This effort has introduced a new dimension to our current view of information systems development: The traditional procedural and technical perceptions of systems development have been enriched by our increasing awareness that equally important human and organizational forces are at work throughout the systems development life cycle.

Part I briefly presented a distillation of the ideas that gave rise to the team approach, and the research techniques that are considered important in maximizing team effectiveness. However, if the potential value of team research is to be fully realized, a bridge is needed between this research and its application. Hence, Part II set out a strategy to apply laboratory-like research to real-world situations.

The strategy required to achieve the desired goals is very clear: First, identify factors that may influence team success and/or failure. Second, identify social science and organizational theory and research relating to those factors. Third, develop a methodology by which the practitioner can apply research results in analyzing and evaluating team performance. Finally, develop practical guidelines for using these observations to improve overall team effectiveness.

While it is always risky to speculate about the future, we feel very confident at this point in saying that the current developments as presented in this book are really a prologue to the future. We believe that there will be an increasingly rapid dissemination of knowledge of and experience with systems development teams and of relevant team research; and furthermore, that this information transfer will assist user and management personnel, as well as systems professionals, in working more effectively in the large-scale systems environment.

We expect to see a growing sophistication in the tools and techniques that are developed to assist practitioners in forming systems development teams, evaluating their performance, diagnosing their problems, and assisting them to function more effectively.

Finally, we anticipate increases in the amount and quality of action research on teams used for information systems development. To some extent, our progress until recently has occurred at an evolutionary pace. That pace will continue to accelerate as new technology is developed to facilitate team development efforts.

For example, increasingly powerful report and screen generators, data dictionary/directory software, and query language capabilities have reduced the burden of programming and other technical tasks associated with systems development. Thus, systems professionals are to some extent becoming more free to engage in meaningful and continuous dialogue with management and users.

As advances continue to accrue, we can envision the systems development team of the future as having available many tools and techniques to improve its systems planning, design, and implementation decisions. If the human and organizational aspects of team development receive at least equal attention and achieve comparable growth, future large-scale development efforts promise to be a striking contrast to the disappointments of the past.

Index

ALSO AVAILABLE FROM YOURDON PRESS

The Practical Guide to Structured Systems Design
by Meilir Page-Jones
368 pages; softcover; 1980
ISBN: 0-917072-17-0

Classics in Software Engineering
Edward Nash Yourdon, Ed.
440 pages; softcover; 1979
ISBN: 0-917072-14-6

Managing the Structured Techniques
by Edward Yourdon
280 pages; softcover; second edition, 1979
ISBN: 0-917072-15-4

Structured Analysis
by Victor Weinberg
344 pages; softcover; 1978
ISBN: 0-917072-07-3

Structured Analysis and System Specification
by Tom DeMarco
368 pages; softcover; 1978
ISBN: 0-917072-07-3

Learning to Program in Structured COBOL, Part 1
by Edward Yourdon, Chris Gane, and Trish Sarson
280 pages; softcover; second edition, 1978
ISBN: 0-917072-12-X

Learning to Program in Structured COBOL, Part 2
by Timothy R. Lister and Edward Yourdon
224 pages; softcover; 1978
ISBN: 0-917072-03-0

For more information on these and other YOURDON texts, write: YOURDON Press, Department PS, 1133 Avenue of the Americas, New York, NY 10036.

YOURDON PRESS MONOGRAPHS

Concise Notes on Software Engineering
by Tom DeMarco
104 pages; softcover; 1979
ISBN: 0-917072-16-2

Structured Walkthroughs
by Edward Yourdon
152 pages; softcover; second edition, 1978
ISBN: 0-917072-09-X

C Notes: A Guide to the C Programming Language
by C.T. Zahn
112 pages; softcover; 1979
ISBN: 0-917072-13-8

For more information on these and other YOURDON texts, write: YOURDON Press, Department PS, 1133 Avenue of the Americas, New York, NY 10036.